Bullies, Bitches and Bastards

Bullies, Bitches and Bastards

(Not so much a book, more a moral crusade)

by
Eileen Condon
and
Amanda Edwards

Illustrations by
Joy Gosney

The Friday Project
An imprint of HarperCollins Publishers
77–85 Fulham Palace Road
Hammersmith, London W6 8JB
www.thefridayproject.co.uk
www.harpercollins.co.uk

First published by The Friday Project in 2008

Copyright © Eileen Condon and Amanda Edwards 2008

1

Eileen Condon and Amanda Edwards assert the moral right to be identified as the authors of this work

A catalogue record for this book is available from the British Library

ISBN 978-1-90-632189-5

All rights reserved. No part of this publication may be reproduced, stored in a retrieval system, or transmitted, in any form or by any means, electronic, mechanical, photocopying, recording or otherwise, without the prior written permission of the publishers.

Designed and typeset by Maggie Dana
Icons by Carrie Kabak
Illustrations by Joy Gosney, www.joygosney.co.uk
Printed and bound in Great Britain by Clays Ltd, St Ives plc

Mixed Sources
Product group from well-managed
forests and other controlled sources
www.fsc.org Cert no. SW-COC-1806
© 1996 Forest Stewardship Council

FSC is a non-profit international organisation established to promote the responsible management of the world's forests. Products carrying the FSC label are independently certified to assure consumers that they come from forests that are managed to meet the social, economic and ecological needs of present or future generations.

Find out more about HarperCollins and the environment at
www.harpercollins.co.uk/green

This book is dedicated to all our family and friends – the perfect antidote to the BBBs out there. (You're not in it. OK!)

All the characters in *Bullies, Bitches and Bastards* are entirely fictitious. Sadly, their behaviour isn't. Furthermore, the authors accept no liability for persons recognising in themselves any of the bullying traits described herein. Quite frankly, if you do – shame on you.

Acknowledgements

We would like to thank Clare, Heather and Scott at The Friday Project for allowing us to vent our spleen. And also Kate Pool at the Society of Authors. Thanks for all your help.

Contents

Introduction ix
   The Git-ometer x

Chapter One   Husbands/Boyfriends 1
   The Enormous Baby Boyfriend 2
   The Moody Bastard 8
   The Man from Atlantis 14
   The Snake Charmer 21
   The 'I'm Not Your Boyfriend' Boyfriend 26

Chapter Two   Wives/Girlfriends 33
   The Interrogator 34
   The Town Crier 39
   The Utter Nutter 45
   The 'What's Yours Is Mine' Girlfriend 52
   The Emasculator 58

Chapter Three   Bosses/Colleagues 63
   Beelzeboss 64
   Work to Ruler 71
   Big Rancour 77

Poacher-turned-Gamekeeper	82
The PG Chimp	88

Chapter Four Family — 95
The Remote Controller	96
Wicked Whittler	101
Me-Me Mum	107
The Toxin-Law	112
The Equaliser	120

Chapter Five Friends — 127
Miss-Fortune Teller	128
Commander-in-Chief	134
The Spadist	140
Mag Hag	146
The Foul Weather Friend	152

Chapter Six Neighbours and Local Folk — 159
Lord of the Manor	160
The Inconvenient Storekeeper	166
The Border Guard	173
Mummy Dearest	179
The Neigh-Boor	185

Conclusion — 191

Introduction

'I have never made but one prayer to God, a very short one: "O Lord, make my enemies ridiculous." And God granted it.' (Voltaire)

That's it. That's enough. They've gone too far. By all that's right and holy, they should be shuffling round a prison yard, shackled by the ankles to a Russian cannibal. But they're not. They're everywhere – people whose characteristics read like a thesaurus of cunning: sly, Machiavellian, gerrymandering, duplicitous, crafty, vulpine.

Bullies. Bitches. Bastards.

Unfortunately, you can't get away from them. They're in your home, in your workplace, and – God help you – even in your bed. And they didn't come with a whiff of sulphur and a tail, did they? Bastards!

You're trapped, doomed, finished – damned to hell in a Hyundai. Hold on: brakes, reverse. There *is* a solution: pin them down, slit them open and dissect them like frogs in a school lab. Not in a vivisectionist way, obviously, but metaphorically speaking.

So here they are, fully exposed: the Snake Charmer, the Utter Nutter, Beelzeboss, the Wicked Whittler, Foul Weather Friend, Lord of the Manor. And that's only a handful of the ... BBBs.

Beggar me backwards! They're ridiculous.

The Git-ometer

The following icons will help you rapidly identify your bullies, your bitches and your bastards. (Oh dear – some have even scored a hat-trick.)

 bully

 bitch

 bastard

Chapter One

Husbands/Boyfriends

The Enormous Baby Boyfriend

What he does

Never grows up. Even if you have babies of your own, he'll be a bigger baby than any of them. At least your proper children will give you intermittent periods of joy and wonder. He won't. He'll whinge, whine, make demands, have moods, inflict sullen silences and throw tantrums. Ultimately, he'll chuck his toys out of the pram and vomit all over you if you don't give him your Full Attention.

His priorities in life? Music, electrical-techno things, money, mates/booze/footie/rugger, socialising (the pub), holidays (snowboarding), DVDs (Tarantino), games (monster-girl-gun-shoot). Oh, and the kids. Anything else? Ermmmmm. Oh yeah! You.

Mooching about in his skateboard gear, he drinks latté in a takeaway cup – with a straw. He will text, text, text, text, text. He'll plug into iMacs, iPods, PSPs, hi-fis and Wi-Fis in the company of friends and family. He will glaze over if the conversation doesn't revolve around him.

When he's not hooked up to a gadget, he will take to his bed for afternoon naps because you and the children 'exhaust' him, and he needs to preserve his energy for… more takeaway coffee and downloading iTunes. He is 42.

That's the age at which people used to die years ago, having led a full, adult life, with all the trimmings: fighting for their country, starting a family at 20, not getting into debt for shiny things and trinkets, being mature enough to realise that once they had children of their own, they had to put away childish things.

Not this one. Even in his early middle age, he still requires a babysitter himself.

If, say, you decided to leave your infants in the care of a 15-year-old youth with a penchant for sinister video games and self-harming, fair enough: you wouldn't be surprised to find *him* splayed out on the sofa while the fruits of your womb are running amok, sticking their fingers into every available socket. This, however, is *not* what you expect when you ask your other half to mind the kids while you take a quick phone call in the bedroom.

Essentially, when you require him to be at his most grown-up, he will let you down worse than any five-year-old denied access to a Wacky Warehouse Christmas free-for-all.

A halogen-downlit office. You, trying to unpack the cargo of verbal nonsense a 19-year-old estate agent is offloading. EBB next to you, head down.

You: ... so, essentially, what you're saying is that the vendors' purchase has fallen through? ... oh, they've found another house? ... but that's in probate, isn't it? ... and doesn't that mean it won't go through for months, if not years? ... but we've sold ours and we're renting on a six-month lease – can we get our solicitor to put pressure on the vendors to go into rented accommodation? ... but then, surely, if we do that, we can at least go ahead with our purchase and not be out of pocket? ... oh, I don't know, I'm not sure I know just what you're advising us to do at this point... *(Turning to EBB)* What do you think?
EBB *(glancing up from his 30GB Apple Video iPod)*: Eh?

It gets worse.

The hallway, you, halfway down the stairs, panting and clasping the rails. EBB lounging in doorway.

You *(calling out)*: What are you doing?
EBB: Why?
You *(exasperated)*: What are you doing?
EBB: Just on the phone to work. Alright?
You: Did you make the other call?
EBB *(irritated)*: What call?
You: To the midwife?
EBB *(into receiver)*: Hold on a minute, I'm getting interrupted this end.

You: Have. You. Rung. The. Midwife?
EBB: I. Am. On. The. Phone.
You (*seizing phone*): Ring her now.
EBB (*wandering off to living room*): You do it. I don't know the number.
You: Where are you going?
EBB: I've got to Sky Plus *Clarkson Goes Large*.

You look at phone, contemplating its use as possible murder weapon, and pondering the chances of getting off with diminished responsibility due to contractions.

What he says

'We need a new one.'
'Give it to me, it's my turn.'
'Boo-hoo.'

What you need to do

Become a fully qualified childminder – you'll need a certificate to hold up in court when he tries to sue you for lack of attention.

Put him in the ballpool at IKEA. He's no good to you when you're trying to decide between the Zuftluft sofa bed and the Zerplerp recliner.

Draw up a reward chart. He gets an extra hour on his Scalextric if he tidies his trainers on the shoe rack; an hour less if he forgets to pick up the kids from school – again.

The Moody Bastard

What he does

Has his emotional barometer set permanently on heavy weather. 'Going into one' is his *raison d'être*. Bought Sainsbury's own-label muesli? Big mood, even though he ate it yesterday. Turned the light switch on too noisily? Big Mood. Breathing in and out too frequently? Big Mood. Someone dies? Big Mood. Someone doesn't die? Big Mood.

Although being extremely tetchy is more or less his full-time occupation, he manages to squeeze in a couple of extracurricular activities: Sending You to Coventry and Stomping Off.

He will Stomp Off anywhere and for no reason whatsoever. He will do it when you're enjoying yourself and when you're not enjoying yourself. Either way, he says it's because he 'doesn't need the hassle'. Even on a pedalo in the middle of the Med, he'd find a way of Stomping Off.

It's as if the Lord God Almighty had a big stick and was prodding him, and him alone, with it. No one on the planet is having a worse time, or is so deeply misunderstood.

But nothing particularly bad has happened to MB – oh, apart from that time you wittily nicked a chip off his plate. *That* sulk lasted a week.

If he worked on the production line in a Prozac factory, he'd still manage to create an atmosphere of despondency. But then that's because MB 'thinks too much', has 'too much depth' and 'was born with a Jack Kerouac temperament'. No, he doesn't. No, he hasn't. And no, he wasn't. He's just a peevish arse whose mission in life is to spoil your fun.

You and MB on sofa. You one end, MB at other, his arms crossed, sighing intermittently.

You: I love *The Simpsons*, don't you?
MB: Yeah. (*Not smiling*) It's funny.
You: I love Apu.
MB: That's *my* favourite character.
You: Hey, snap!
MB: I thought you liked Marge.
You: No. Apu.
MB: Hang on! You definitely said you liked Marge.
You: I *do* like her but my favourite is Apu.
MB: I don't believe this. You only like Apu because I said I did.
You: I did not. I've always liked Apu.
MB: I liked Apu first. I liked Apu before you were born.
You: It doesn't matter.
MB: Yes, it does because you always have to spoil everything. If I like something, then you like it. Can't I just like something,

without you liking it, for God's sake? Just let me have something for myself, will you? Haven't you got a mind of your own? Let's just watch *Location, Location, Location*. You've ruined this entire episode.

Even a shopping trip can turn into a minefield.

A supermarket. You, standing by the lollo rosso, MB next to you, arms folded, sighing.

MB: What are you doing?
You: Just squeezing these lettuces to see if they're fresh.
MB: Why are you squeezing every third one?
You: I just am.
MB: Just squeeze the first.
You: What?
MB: Just squeeze the first one or the second one. You don't have to do the third one.
You: There aren't any rules for squeezing lettuces.
MB: So, in that case, why are you doing every third one? You've just completely contradicted yourself. You always have to be right, don't you?
You: How can I contradict myself *and* always be right?
MB: You'd find a way.
You: Look, I'm not going to have a row with you about squeezing lettuces.

MB: In that case, stop picking an argument.
You: I didn't! *You* started it.
MB: God, how childish. 'You started it.'
You: I can't say anything, can I? Just... stop being in such a mood.
MB: Do you bloody wonder why I get in a mood with you around? Just get a courgette. I couldn't eat that lettuce now, thanks to your ridiculous behaviour. (*Stomping Off to Cereals*)

Everyone around MB ends up comparing their antidepressant dosages and side effects. He, however, has never taken a pill in his life. Why would he? Being surly is his greatest joy.

What he says

'I'm mercurial, like the moon. I cannot help my overwhelming emotions.'

'You ruin everything.'

'No, I don't want a bloody cup of tea!'

What you need to do

Learn to enjoy the sound of silence. There will be a lot – interspersed with heavy sighing.

Change his ringtone from *Heaven Knows, I'm Miserable Now* to *Walking on Sunshine*.

Don't let him bring you down – you keep up with your career as a cheerleader.

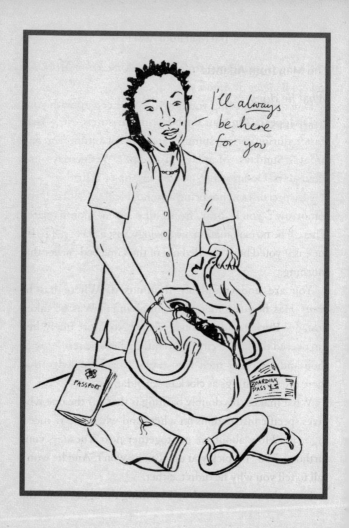

The Man from Atlantis

What he does

Disappears. On your birthday, at Christmas, New Year, Easter, during spring, summer and most of autumn, on Saturdays, Sundays, Mondays, Tuesdays, Wednesdays and Thursdays. Occasionally, he will turn up on a Friday.

He specialises in not being around. He'll say, 'I'll call you tomorrow'; you'll hear from him seven months later. There'll be no explanation, no apology, just a cheery, 'Hi. It's me', as if you'd both crawled out of the same bed earlier that morning.

You are understandably flummoxed. Where has he *been*? Has he just emerged from a coma? Was he taken hostage? Buried under a ton of silage? No. More likely, he's discovered the fabled city of Atlantis, where he resides with thousands of other men who refuse to acknowledge that there are such things as clock or calendar.

What makes this doubly baffling is that *he's* the one who gives specific instructions on where and when you're meeting, e.g., 'How about we get together next Tuesday, your birthday, 7.30? I'll pick you up.' But he won't. And he won't call to tell you why he didn't, either.

So you're tortured with self-loathing thoughts along the

lines of 'Did I bore him?', 'Do I make him sick?', 'Have I got too much to say for myself?', 'Am I, as my mother always warned me, too independent for my own good?', 'I made him laugh, they don't like that', 'Did I spend enough time making him feel good about himself?', 'Is it my saddlebags, my Primark pants, my wonky fringe?', 'Do I look like the lead singer of Kiss?'

Once you've canvassed the opinions of every member of your family and your entire circle of friends and come to the realisation that you are not so awful someone would rather fake his own death than see you again, you take charge.

You fill up the blank dates in your diary that you were keeping open in hope for him. Finally, ultimately, *hallelujahly*, you delete every technological trace of him. That's when your mobile will ring, up will flash the familiar number, 'Hey, how are you doing?' and here we bloody well go again.

Still, how can you stay cross at him? You love the fact that he's bohemian, romantic, a free spirit, unfettered by the demands of time, an international man of mystery. Stuff that. This 'free spirit' is free to do what he likes, when he likes, where he likes, with no thought for you.

While the rest of us stick to our commitments and, at the very least, offer an apology if we have to let someone down,

MfA just sticks one finger up at your plans and boots your hopes and dreams squarely up the backside.

His constant disappearing acts mess with your mind. You receive a text: *I will see you tomorrow at 8.* Of course, he doesn't show. You start to wonder if *I will see you tomorrow at 8* bears an encrypted meaning and you haven't cracked the code. Finally, you will start to think you've made him up. He's a hallucination; he's your imaginary boyfriend. Sadly, he's for real, and a complete cock.

You, holding court at Casa Felafel, surrounded by 23 of your closest friends. Your mobile lights up with his number.

MfA: Can I take you to dinner next week?
You: Lovely. When? Where?
MfA (*very decisively*): La Romantica. 7.30.
You: Great! See you there.
MfA: I'll ring you on the day.

Three weeks later, after you've given yourself a dry-eye condition from scanning the railway tracks for bodies, your mobile again lights up.

MfA: Hi. It's me. How are you?
You (*glancing at your packet of herbal memory booster pills*):
    Erm ... fine. You?

MfA: Couldn't be better. Listen, when can we meet up? Are you free this week?
You (*hesitant*): Yeah, should be.
MfA: Great, it'd be lovely to see you. Let's say Thursday. I could come to you.
You: Okay, what time?
MfA: Eight-ish. I'll ring you on the day.

Ad infinitum. Ad infinitum.

On those rare occasions when you *do* actually meet, and even enjoy an idyllic date, naturally you'll assume he feels the same as you, therefore rendering further Vanishing Acts obsolete. Don't count on it.

You and MfA wander out of a cinema foyer, a crescent moon suddenly revealing itself from behind a cloud, the Thames shimmering glitteringly, a laughing breeze softly lifting your hair. MfA gathers you up in his arms and waltzes you round the passers-by, who look on sentimentally.

MfA (*cupping your face in his hands*): I've had a wonderful time today.
You: Really?
MfA: Mmmm. You're everything I want in a woman – smart, beautiful. I don't like spending any time away from you.

The Man from Atlantis

You: Really?
MfA: Mmmmm ... Don't leave me, will you?
You: I'm not going anywhere. (*He is, though*)
MfA: I want to see more and more of you.
You: Really?
MfA: I'll call you first thing tomorrow.
You: Really?

Weeks and weeks later, when your mobile has sprouted a beard, you see him again, nonchalantly strolling out of Chelsea stadium into your path.

MfA: Oh, hi! My team's just won. How are you? Are you free next week?
You: Erm ...
MfA: Great, say about 8? I'll ring you on the day.

What he says

'I'll call you Wednesday.' He won't.
'I'll come straight over.' He won't.
'I'll always be here for you.' He won't. He just won't.

What you need to do

Go on a missing persons website and take your pick from the list. You'll have a much more fulfilling relationship, and at least you'll know where you stand with someone who really *has* disappeared.

Book a holiday to the Bermuda Triangle. It'll be a lot easier finding that than him.

Tag him.

The Snake Charmer

What he does

Sheds his cashmere jumper and jumbo cord trews to reveal the snakeskin beneath, the minute he's got you where he wants you. While other men stampede shrieking from commitment, he's in like Flynn. No sooner have you added his name to 'My Numbers', than you're flashing his engagement ring.

He must *really* love you. Oh yeah, like a farmer loves his branded cow. The only time he's ever serenaded you it was with *The Python's Song* from *The Jungle Book*.

You were an intelligent, independent woman: you used to book priority seating online at easyJet; you were known to pick up the *FT*, peruse it and understand a smidgen of it; you could even take a conference call while simultaneously pacing the room with an air of self-importance.

Since when did you add 'must become a chattel' to your 'life list'? Since he turned from charmer to snake – which was midway through the wedding reception, when he took you to one side, kissed you tenderly on the cheek and told you, 'You look beautiful. Don't wear your hair up again.'

Your instinct was screaming, 'Pick up the hem of your meringue, grab a bottle of cava and get the hell out!' But the reasoning part of your brain was telling you, 'Don't be ridiculous, this man is perfect. He always says and does the right thing.'

Course he does. He graduated from charm school with honours, has an MA in mesmerism, and a PhD in swallowing mice whole. Before the handover, sorry, wedding, he never put a foot wrong: 'It doesn't matter that it's been three hours; I could listen to you for three more'; 'Tell me again about your ex-boyfriends. All of them'; 'Would you like me to organise flowers for your mum for Mother's Day while I'm at the florist's at lunchtime?'

What's not to marry?

A balmy day in July. Squirrels are squirrelling, birds are twittering, the late afternoon sun slants through the willows' frail fronds. You and SC recline on a Cath Kidston picnic rug, while champagne flutes gently fizz and strawberries are exchanged lip to lip. Aaaaaahh.

SC (*to mother with baby passing by*): They're so lovely at that age, aren't they?

You sigh blissfully.

SC (*to elderly couple passing by*): Glorious weather, isn't it? Lovely day for a stroll.

You emit a heavenly sigh.

SC leans back on Cath Kidston, turns, and looks at you intently for some moments.

You (*smiling expectantly*): What?
SC: Your eyes. Never noticed them before.
You (*still smiling expectantly*): What about them?
SC: No, I've just never noticed them before.
You (*crestfallen*): Oh.

A New Year's Eve bash in full swing: champagne fizzing, the moonlight slanting through the Georgian windows, a Cath Kidston throw adorns the chaise longue, etc., etc.

SC (*to your best friend*): Is that Arôme de la Recherche du Temps Perdu? Thought so. Once smelt, never forgotten. And that dress is *definitely* your blue.

Friend floats away on a cloud of compliments.

You: I've got something in that blue. I could wear it to your brother's party.
SC: Yeah right. You'd look like a pig in it.
You (*crestfallen*): Oh.

A crowded, festive restaurant: champagne fizzing, candlelight casting slanting shadows across the table. (No Cath Kidston here; it's oriental minimalism.)

You: ... what would make sense would be if the developing

countries were allowed to increase their CO_2 emissions, while the richer nations cut back drastically on theirs and eventually you'd have a balance ...
SC: Hark at thicket! Just kidding.

Embarrassed silence and sidelong glances all round.

Mission accomplished: next time you're in Robert Dyas, customers will have a hard time distinguishing between you and the doormats. Charming!

What he says

'What's *your* problem?' (You.)
'What's the matter with you?' (You.)
'What are you so miserable about?' (You. You. YOU!)

What you need to do

Keep an eye on the Ali Baba laundry basket – he could pop up at any moment.

Arrange a dinner party with his work colleagues (he hasn't got any close friends). Get yourself drunk. 'Accidentally' blurt out: 'Do you lot all know he's got breasts? Real ones, it's not just fat. Go on, show them.'

Actually, just leave him.

The 'I'm Not Your Boyfriend' Boyfriend

What he does

Insists continually that what you have is a casual relationship – even if you were both standing in front of a vicar intoning, 'Love is never boastful, nor conceited, nor rude; never selfish.' (Ahem.) In his head, he's a single man. Well, you never know – something better might come along.

For now, though, there's you. With a few provisos: he doesn't do holidays, mini-breaks, dinner parties, birthdays, cinema or the theatre. He may occasionally do the pub, but won't do restaurants, and he definitely doesn't do Sunday lunch with your parents.

This man would rather stand in a crowded market in Basra than have a discussion about Where He Sees the Relationship Going. You have now 'not being going out' for five years – five years that could better have been spent with someone who doesn't mind being seen out with you, actually enjoys your company, tells you (*whisper it now*) he loves you, and would like to be instrumental in fertilising your diminishing egg stock.

Oh, to meet *him*. Fat chance. The second INYBB sees your eyes wandering, he will dangle the carrot of commitment. 'Let's go round Asda together next Saturday.' 'Shall we call into Homebase and look at gazebos?' 'Oh, hold on a minute, have you seen this? Two beds, a garage, a garden *and* local amenities.'

Don't get carried away – none of the above will happen. The 'we're not going out' clause is still firmly in the contract. So, back to solo holidays, solitary walks, separate nights out and soliloquies.

The most you'll get from your 'boyfriend' is an email telling you how much he's missing you while you're trekking the Machu Picchu trail on your lonesome. Or he'll text *Do you fancy coming over later?* while you're out with your friends, and then hide with the lights off when you do actually turn up at his door.

INYBB excuses his fear of commitment by mentioning that the last time he got serious, his ex was sectioned when he called it off. (The implication being that he's so adorable women go mad if they can't have him.) Track that girl down. She probably went nuts because of his constant on/off, push me/pull me nonsense.

Honestly, you'd think he was a playboy, having far too much fun to ditch it all for a wife and a semi in Welwyn Garden City. But INYBB lives alone, in a bleak flat, with a single divan and his pants and socks stuck to the radiator. What a catch.

The 'I'm Not Your Boyfriend' Boyfriend

You, strolling through T.K. Maxx, fingering the merchandise. Your phone rings.

INYBB: Hi! It's me.
You: Oh, hello. You don't usually ring *me*. What's wrong?
INYBB (*rashly*): Look ... listen ... erm ... what it *is* is someone gave me this voucher ... buy one meal, get the second free at Izzzi's ... whatdyathink?
You (*incredulously*): What, *us* going?
INYBB (*nervously*): Well, yeah. Us. (*Oh God. Us!*)
You: Great. Yeah. Fantastic!
INYBB (*starting to shake*): Yeah ... great ... fantastic ... yeah ... er ...
You: Tonight! Is it for tonight?
INYBB: Erm ... (*looking at voucher*) just checking ... actually ... wait a minute, what's the date here?
You (*quickly*): Doesn't matter, let's just go anyway. What time?
Silence.
You: Hi? Are you still there?
INYBB: I think ... what's the date today? What does it say here? Something about ...
You (*disappointed*): Oh, is there a cut-off date?
INYBB (*like a flash*): Yesss! Found it ... here it is ... it was yesterday ... oh dear.

Say he does have a more severe lapse of concentration

and – mercy me! – finds himself walking through a park with you. In front of other people.

You, strolling along with INYBB, slipping your arm happily through his and sighing.

You: So, do you fancy doing something tonight? Seems a shame to go home after such a lovely afternoon.
INYBB: Erm, well, I've got to get up early.
You: I wasn't planning on staying over.
INYBB (*Phew!*): It's just that I need to prepare that pitch.
You: What pitch? You're an electrician.
INYBB: Just a bit exhausted.
You: Okay, well, how about I cook us something nice, get a DVD and then head home?
INYBB: Erm ... oh look! A squirrel.
You: Shall I then?
INYBB: What?
You: Do what I just said?
INYBB: Look, I think we should just slow this down. It's all going a bit too fast. (*Running to the car park*) We should just calm it down a bit. (*Shouting through the car window as the tyres squeal away through the gates*) I JUST NEED A BIT OF SPACE!

The 'I'm Not Your Boyfriend' Boyfriend

What he says

'Okay, I'll see you Friday night but it's just two friends watching a DVD, then having sex and then you going home.'

'Okay, I'll move in, but it's only until I've rewired my place. It doesn't mean we're in a relationship.'

'Okay, I'll drop you off at your house, but it's a one-off.'

What you need to do

Turn the screws on him: take him to John Lewis and make him browse the haberdashery department. Watch him turn ashen.

Freak him out good and proper by bringing your six-year-old niece on a date and asking him, 'Do you think *we'd* make good parents?'

Just tell him you really *are* 'not going out' with him. See ya!

Chapter Two
Wives/Girlfriends

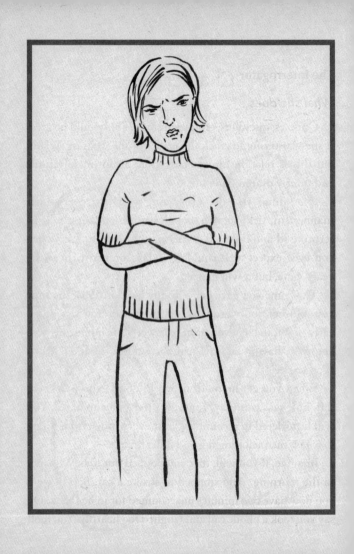

The Interrogator

What she does

Quizzes, questions, cross-examines. This would be great if she was trying to crack the leader of the Tooting Triads, but this is relationship interrogation: an ultimately futile and utterly draining pursuit.

Everything you do, everything you say, every little mannerism, tick, scratch, cough, sniffle and sigh will be scrutinised and digested, to be spat out in your face when you least expect it. It could be today, tomorrow or in six years' time, but it will happen.

That time you gave her a 'funny look' in 1994, the time you told her you were too tired to see her and having an early night, the day you didn't answer your mobile because you were having an MRI scan – it's all in the file marked 'Vengeance'.

When you get home from work, don't expect a cheery 'Hi, how was your day?' and the offer of a cup of tea. You will be ordered to account for your every move from 8 a.m. to 6.43 p.m., including fag and toilet breaks.

Imagine, if you will, that you popped out to buy a paper in the morning. And stopped to stroke a cat. Bad move – you now have two minutes unaccounted for in her book. Or, say you took a phone call and laughed too heartily. You fool!

You now have to explain for the next four hours why you don't laugh like that with *her*.

Carelessly, you chat to a woman at a function you and TI are both attending. Are you *demented*? You may as well tie yourself to a kitchen chair, put *Stuck in the Middle with You* on the CD player and beat yourself repeatedly around the face with a wet tea towel.

Don't bother complaining that your post has been tampered with, your computer's been hacked into and your phone calls are being bugged. It's her. Making sure you're doing what you're supposed to be doing, *when* you're supposed to be doing it, *where* you're supposed to be doing it, and with *whom*.

It's no accident her DVD library comprises box sets of *Judge John Deed*, *Crown Court*, *Rumpole of the Bailey*, *Prime Suspect* and *Alice in Wonderland* (that Queen of Hearts, she was on the knave's case).

You and TI side by side in the Multiplex.

You (*thoroughly relaxed*): Do you want a Malteser?
TI (*whispering*): Why did you wear that brown suit last Friday?
You: Whaat?
TI (*whispering urgently*): Last Friday. The brown suit. You normally wear the grey.

The Interrogator 37

You (*through gritted teeth*): What are you on about? I'm trying to watch the film.
TI (*whispering furiously*): Did you actually go to work?
You: Course I did, where do you think I went?
TI (*hissing loudly*): You tell me.
You (*quietly*): Let's Just Watch the Film.
TI (*out loud*): Not until I have a straight answer from you.

Much shushing from assembled cinemagoers.

You: I don't know. I probably wore the brown suit because the grey one was dirty.
TI: How did it get dirty? It was only dry cleaned last Wednesday.
You: I don't *know*. Things get stained.
TI (*shouting*): Stained! Stained! (*Standing up*) YOU BASTARD!

She's not your girlfriend, she's your stalker. You're constantly looking over your shoulder. And that's just in the kitchen. When she comes out of the ensuite at lights-out time, you're not lying in a come-hither pose, you're curled up in the foetal position at the bottom of the duvet.

Your relationship is a trial. Literally. And she's the self-appointed judge, juror and jailer. You're insecure, anxious, paranoid. Sitting at the Formica kitchen table as she strides the room, you cry out, 'What have I done? What have I done wrong?'

'Everything.'

Interview terminated 12.04 a.m. Suspect not cooperating.

What she says

'You know how to whistle, don't you? By the time I've finished with you, you'll be whistling like a canary. You're a wisecracking, dumb ass sonofabitch and you don't know shit from Shinola. All you're giving me is sketchy details, but you've come in here with dirty hands, a lot to hide. Get me a steno pad. Call it a hunch, but you're going to spill. I'm onto you, punk.'

'I'm not one to read into things.'

What you need to do

Next time she grills you, come over all Beckettian. Ask her exactly what she means by 'Where?' counter her question 'What are you doing?' with an existential riposte, 'Hmmm, "doing", are we *anything* when we are not "doing"?' And as to her constant 'Who were you with?' reply enigmatically, 'Do you mean in the corporeal sense? Or are we talking metaphorically?'

The Town Crier

What she does

Spends so much time bawling, it's a wonder she doesn't drown. Your whole relationship is a snivel and phlegm fest. She's just so sensitive. Actually, she's not. She's more expert at manipulation than a chiropractor.

How's this for sensitive? She can flirt with your best friend, run down your job, and denigrate your family but if at any point you raise the slightest objection, you'll get instant waterworks and, 'Boo hoo, why are you always so mean to me?' And if she can do it in public, so much the better.

You on barstool, flicking beer mat. TC on stool next to you, inspecting fingernails.

You: Do you want another drink?
TC: No.
You: Shall we go home then?
TC: I'm here with my friends.
You (*sighing*): Is this about Christmas?
TC: What about Christmas?
You: Look. My mum's not well. She'd love to see all the family this year. We've always been away, this is just one year when I'd like to do the family thing. It's not much to ask.

TC: I want a holiday. I need to get away. Your sister can look after your mum.

You: That's not fair – she's got the girls. Besides, I want to see my mum.

TC (*imitating whiny toddler*): 'I wanna see my mum.' Oh grow up.

You: That's out of order. You're being really selfish. You can forget about going on holiday now.

TC starts to cry, as friends emerge from dark corners and flock around, twittering, 'Oh my God, what's up?' 'Are you alright?' 'Oh sweetheart, ahhh, don't get upset, has he made you cry?'

TC: I don't want to talk about it. He's just called me a selfish bitch. (*Gasps from friends, accusing eyes on you*)

You: I'm really sorry ... I didn't say bitch ... I ... just ...

TC: *Sob*. But. *Sob*. You. *Sob*. Said. *Sob*. I. *Sob*. Was. *Sob*. Selfish. *Sob sob*.

You: I didn't mean it. I'm sorry, I didn't mean to upset you. Let's go home. (*Now. Quickly. Away from the baying mob*)

Whoever gave her Tiny Tears as a child didn't realise she was going to use the doll as her role model for the rest of her life. If only scientists could figure out a way of regulating the ebb and flow of water as deftly as she does, East Anglia would breathe a sigh of relief.

You will soon learn never to thwart her. Because if you do, she will wield the water torture. You, the kind-hearted gent that you are, will be struggling to come to terms with the fact that all you ever do is make your girlfriend cry.

You awful, unfeeling, callous bastard. But wait – think about it. The tears are for you and you alone. Funny how she can sit granite-faced as a friend tells her about a heart-breaking love split, or remain unmoved and dry-eyed through TV scenes of famine and war. But then she would, because there's absolutely nothing in it for her if she blubbers over starving orphans.

Crying isn't an indication of her empathy with the suffering of humanity. Crying is control. And if she hasn't got her own tragedy to use as a weapon against you, she'll just hijack someone else's.

You and TC in bed; you reading, TC, back to you, huffing.

You (*resignedly*): You OK?

TC huffs.

You (*placing book down*): I am *not* driving all the way to Inverness in one day.

TC huffs.

You: It's ridiculous. If we take the sleeper, we can make an adventure of it, we arrive fresh ...

TC huffs.

You: ... we'll have the whole day to ourselves. *I* won't be knackered from driving. And anyway, the weather's rubbish – we wouldn't even be able to have the soft top down ...

TC huffs.

You (*cuddling up to TC's back, murmuring*):.. overnight sleeper, could be really romantic ...

TC (*flinging your arm away*): I don't believe this. You *know* why I don't like trains (*lip trembling*) ... I can't believe (*voice wobbling*) you've forgotten (*full-on wailing*) MY MUM'S NEIGHBOUR'S CLEANER WAS KILLED IN A TRAIN CRAAAAASH! Waaaaaaah!

You: I'll check the tyres tomorrow.

You're genetically programmed to wince when a woman blubs; she knew this from the age of five. You don't stand a chance – it's all going to end in tears. Yours.

What she says

'Whaaaaaaaa ... whaaaaaaaa/blub/sob/whimper/bawl/snivel/roar.'

'Whaaaaaa ... whaaaaa/snivel/blub/roar/bawl/sob.'
'Whaaaaa ... whaaaaaa/roar/snivel/sob/blub.'

What you need to do

Go on a 'Big Boys do Cry' seminar. Wallow in the wailing. Now it's *your* turn to let rip with the tear ducts. Over everything. From ikkle baby shoes to Westlife videos.

Take out shares in Gore-Tex.

Hope she drowns.

The Utter Nutter

What she does

Arranges her soft toys amidst the 43 carefully positioned cushions, pillows and bolsters on her bed. Twinkling fairy lights are threaded through the Victoriana iron bedstead, aromatic candles waft from every available surface, her dressing table is festooned with jewelled scent bottles, pink potions and powder puffs. Delightful! It's *Move Over, Darling*. It's 1963. She's Doris Day!

No she isn't. She's Kathy Bates. It's *Misery*. All round. You get lured in by the frippery and frou-frou. Here's a girl who's the perfect recipient of your protective masculine instincts. She needs a good looking after. (Yes, she does. But in a secure environment, with people far more medically qualified than you. That's for later.)

For now, you're in. Although you do have one little niggle. The bichon frise that's always under her arm can apparently 'talk' and 'understands' her. Girls, eh? What can you do?

A few months further down the line, and you're beginning to think the talking dog was the least of your worries. You take her on holiday with your brother and his wife. UN thinks the 16-year-old bellboy 'looks like a rapist'. So she remains in her room. For the entire four days.

Now you're nervous about this relationship, plus you're not getting invited to your brother's any more. Or your mum's, come to that, or your best mate's, or your sister's. Or even that bloke from the pub's.

She's not that bad, really. She's an emotional girl. All women are emotional, aren't they? This emotional?

You, on the phone, feet up on desk, leaning back in chair, scratching your chest absently.

You: Yeah, no worries, that order will be with you by the 20th.
   Ha, ha, yeah, everything's fine at this ...
UN (*to a security guard*): GET YOUR HANDS OFF ME!
You: Sorry, gonna have to go.
UN: YOU CAN'T STOP ME TALKING TO MY BOYFRIEND!
You: What's wrong darling? What's going on? What's happening? Is it the car?
UN: YOU LYING ... WHO IS SHE?
You (*muttering*): Let's go outside and just calm down.
UN: CALM DOWN! CALM DOWN! Who is she? Who *is* she?
You: There isn't a 'she'. We've been over this. There's only you.
   It's all in your head.
UN: YOU LIAR. YOU LIAR!
You: Please, darling. This is not the place.

UN: So it's true. I knew it. OH MY GOD. (*Slumps to the office floor, sobbing and wailing*)
You: Errrrmmm ... err ... does anyone know what floor the sick room's on?

We're moving swiftly on now, past Knutsford, beyond Nut Bush City Limits.

You, jolted out of sleep by the sound of wardrobe doors crashing, drawers being yanked open as a shadowy figure you blearily recognise as UN whirlwinds round the room and heads for the door.

You: What are you doing? It's three in the morning.
UN: Did you go to sleep?! I was talking to you.
You: Where are you going?
UN: If you think I can spend another minute in that bed ...
You: Come back, for God's sake.

Front door slams.

You (*wearily*): Ohhhhh Godddddd ... I'm going to have to go and get her. (*Five minutes later, you, sockless, coat over pyjamas, driving at 15mph through torrential rain and gale-force winds, scanning the pavements for a woman in her nightie and slippers. UN, stumbling along asymmetrically, one foot in, one foot out of the gutter.*)

You (*to yourself*): Oh God, there she is. (*To her*) Come on, get in the car, you're soaked through. What *is* this all about?
UN (*melodramatically*): You don't know, do you?
You (*helplessly*): No. I ... don't. I actually don't.
UN: If you think I'm getting in that car ...
You: Please just get in the car.

UN slumps against lamppost, sobbing and wailing.

And here we go into the Seventh Circle of Hell.

You, whistling your way up the garden path, looking forward to shepherd's pie and a tankard of Crooked Bishop. Suddenly spotting smashed DVD player on the lawn.

You: What the ...? (*Spying the TV up-ended in the flowerbed*) What ...? (*Contemplating your trousers flapping from the Sky dish*) Whaaaat the ...? (*Walking through the front door, surveying a scene of grotesque devastation. UN standing amidst the debris, arms folded, staring at you*)
You: Oh my God, we've been burgled. Have you called the police? Are you okay? When did it happen? Were you here? Are you okay?
UN: You were supposed to call me this morning.
You: I did. You weren't here.
UN: I was here. Why didn't you call me back?
You (*looking anew at trashed home. Click!*): Ah, err, listen ...

(*Walking tentatively towards her*) Well ... Well ... why don't you tell me in future the time you'd like me to ring ... (*Moving gently closer*) I'll always ring at that time ... (*A step nearer*) What time would suit you? (*Lightly cupping hand under UN's left elbow*) Should we say ... eleven? Ish?

UN suddenly, violently, raining fists upon your chest, before flying out front door. You slump to floor, head in hands.

You try to leave her. She threatens to kill herself. Every day. Six months later she's still alive and kicking. Finally, you make a run for it while she's away leading a Negotiating Skills workshop.

Seven months later, you, on phone, feet on desk, leaning back, scratching neck absently.

You: Yeah mate, feeling a lot better, doctor reckons I can reduce the dose gradually. No, no idea, haven't seen her for ...
UN (*to a security guard*): GET YOUR HANDS OFF ME!!!

What she says

'I'm not paranoid. I know you're always talking about me.'

'I mean it. I'm really going to do it this time.'

'Hi, it's me ...' (One year after you've assumed a new identity.) 'Hi. Me again.' (Two years after you've moved to a safe house.) 'Hi, long time no see.' (Four years after you've had plastic surgery.)

What you need to do

Emigrate.

The 'What's Yours Is Mine' Girlfriend

What she does

Behaves as if she's the daughter of Messrs Sketchley and Co. – she doesn't just take you to the cleaner's, she jet hoses, sandblasts and puts you through the mangle. Then she hangs you out to dry.

In the early days of romance, she's not gazing at you, hands clasped across a table for ages ... And ages ... And ages ... She has no use for that – there's research to be done. She's studying your asset portfolio: i.e., your salary, your home, your car, your bonus, your PEPs, your pension, your ISAs, your Wesley-Barrell four-seater sofa, your fixtures, your fittings, and the snow globe you got when you were five (might be worth a bit on eBay).

Who needs a proper job? She's already head of acquisitions and mergers: she merges with you and acquires what you've got. That's the foundation upon which she's built her 'career'.

Her mission statement has always been: 'What's Yours is Mine'. They were probably the first words she uttered. Other little girls were enchanted by the story of Cinderella's marriage to the prince – so was she. But only because WYIMG realised it meant Cinders got to keep half the castle. And they all lived happily ever after.

She didn't spend her teenage years hanging around the waltzers, lusting after the carneys; *she* was over at the circus hunting down Mr Billy Smart to see how many spare sons he had and what was their percentage stake in the business.

Romance has never come into it. The only way you'll woo her is if you lay your cards (credit, debit, Visa, gold, etc.) firmly on the table. If the figures balance in her favour, you may, just may, see a flicker of attraction.

You, absorbed in a three-foot-high leather-bound menu, WYIMG, absorbed by a glimpse of your Rolex.

You: Are you having a dessert?

WYIMG: Hmm? So are you actually based in the City?

You: All over the place, really – City, New York, Shanghai. Think I'll have the lemon torte ...

WYIMG: Ooh. Busy. Don't understand any of it myself. I haven't got a clue about money. I wouldn't even know where to start with a pension ...

You: I could always take a look if you like. Do you fancy another Prosecco?

WYIMG: Oh, would you? Do you mind? Well, you're the expert, company director and all that. (*Suddenly pulling low-cut top down even lower, 'Look at these and tell me how much you earn ... Now!'*) I bet you're up there in the six-figure bracket ...

The 'What's Yours Is Mine' Girlfriend

You: Mmmm, well ... I dunno ... maybe ... on paper ... Should I get another bottle?

WYIMG: More than a hundred K? Or higher? Lower? Ha ha.

You: Brucie! *Play Your Cards Right*! Ha ha.

WYIMG: No. Is it? Higher? Or lower?

You (*slightly embarrassed*): Higher. Yeah, higher. I'm definitely having another glass. Are you?

WYIMG: Not for me.

You (*smacking lips*): Mmmm-mmm. This is really nice. (*Examines label on bottle*) Well ...

WYIMG (*hoisting up bra and contents*): I bet you've got a lot of it tied up in property. (*Come on! It's getting late*)

You: I've got a couple of places here and I'm looking to buy in France.

WYIMG: Really! Oh, I can just see you there. You actually do have something of a Gallic charm.

You: Oh, I don't know about that.

WYIMG: Yes, definitely. A touch of Olivier Martinez.

You: Well, funnily enough that's not the first time ...

WYIMG: But do you know where I could *really* see you? (*Italy. Because that's where I want to be*)

You: Where?

WYIMG: Italy. There's something very *Dolce Vita* about you.

You: Gosh.

WYIMG: I adore Italy. I could live there tomorrow.

You: It is rather *splendido*. Tad more expensive on the property front, though.
WYIMG: Worth it in the long run. Maybe something to think about. (*Singing*) La la la la la la la la la la big pizza pie, that's (*looking at you*) *amore*.
You: You've got a beautiful voice. Maybe it *should* be the Italian connection, not the French, after all. (*Raises glass*) Cheers!
WYIMG: Just popping to the little girls' room. *Ciao*!
You: *Ciao*.

Don't flatter yourself that she'll stop at nothing to get you; she'll stop at nothing to get what you have. Obstacles — such as a current girlfriend, wife, and children — will merely be swept aside.

Despite the best efforts of friends advising you 'not to go there', inevitably you will find yourself stepping in time to Mendelssohn's *Wedding March*. Make the most of the day, treasure every moment of it. Because once her signature is on that register, you're in big trouble.

Till death us do part? Till wealth us do part, more like. You will be alone in the honeymoon suite, consoling yourself with the chocolates off her pillow because she's already scarpered. And she's in the process of obtaining three quotes for removals (just your stuff) while simultaneously finalising the arrangements for her *next* engagement party.

When you do get back 'home' there's a lawyer waiting on your welcome mat, telling you you've been evicted. That's when you find yourself hunkering down on a park bench, wondering where it all went wrong. And even then she'll demand half the coat you're wearing. (The half without the cider stains.)

What she says

'Ker-ching!!'

'That's mine. And that and that and that and that and that and that and that and that and that and that and that.'

'I'll take a cheque.'

What you need to do

Send her to the Klondike. She'll be so good at panhandling, the others will have to give up and go strawberry picking. She's found her true vocation.

Tell her you've given all your worldly goods to the newly-formed Church of the Heavenly Three Lions (Founder: Wayne Rooney).

Do a Jérôme Kerviel and bring down the bank you're working for. Make sure she's an accessory after the fact.

The Emasculator

What she does

Holds your plums in her palm. But not in an erotic way. The talons are digging in. You couldn't be more emasculated if you were standing in your local farmers' market in a loincloth with a board round your neck reading 'Eunuch'.

Initially, she appeals to the Christopher Robin in you – the little boy who just wants to be tucked in, pecked on the cheek, and bossed into eating his greens, preferably by a bosomy nanny.

And when she does get really cross with you, so much the better – you love it when they're angry.

Don't get excited. This isn't anger with a saucy wink – this is hatred. You're not going to get mollycoddling from 'nanny'. What you *are* going to get is shouted at, ordered about and demeaned. A lot.

A residential avenue, quiet, until now, as your car revs, kangaroos and stalls up and down the road.

TE: Not *here*! Park it further up.

You park the car 100 metres further up.

TE: Oh, well done, near a tree. How am I supposed to get out?

You: Sorry, I was trying to avoid the drain.

TE: How could anyone *not* see a tree?

You: The drain's quite big, you might ...

TE: Hurry UP. What are you doing *now*? Where are you *going*? First gear! FIRST GEAR!

You: I'm trying to reverse, to avoid the tree and the drain ...

TE (*barking*): We will be in this car all day if you don't sort this out and *park it!* Handbrake! HANDBRAKE!! Right. Pass me my bags. Not *that* one. I need my *handbag*. (*Clicking fingers*) Brush.

You: Toothbrush? Hairbrush? Dog brush?!

TE (*looking at you, murderously*): Hair. Brush.

You (*eagerly*): Here it is! Found it!

TE (*brushing hair vigorously, spraying dandruff in your direction*): I'll want my coat. There! On the back seat. Careful! Don't lean over me! I tell you what, here's an idea, why don't you open your door, get out, open the back door, reach in and get my coat? (*Grabbing it from you*) Try *not* to crease it. (*Holds out brush*) Here. Close the door, there's a draught. (*Applying lipstick in rear view mirror before shouting through closed window at you*) What are you *doing*? Open the *door*. *My* door. God. (*Gets out, stalks off, then turns round sharply*) GET THE BAGS!

You trot behind, wheeling overnight bag, handbag in crook of arm, vanity case in teeth.

The Emasculator

You weren't always a castrato. Back in the day, you could hold forth in Pizza Express, without finding her hand clamped across your mouth while telling the assembled guests, 'Don't listen to him. What does he know?'

You once knew Ronaldo's every ball control movement. Now the only footie players you ever watch are the ones doing the American Smooth on *Strictly Come Prancing*.

When you get the builders in to do the extension, she's the one in the hard hat with the architect's plans, while you're trolling down to SaveuLike to buy cheap teabags and eight kilos of white sugar.

This can't go on. Your testosterone gauge is so low it's beeping at you to refuel. Time to make a stand.

You, looking in hallway mirror, mouthing defiant words, before bursting through lounge door. TE, sitting on sofa, watching television.

You (*hurriedly*): I was thinking of going fishing on Saturday.
TE (*without looking round*): No, you're not.
You (*moving round the sofa to stand in her eyeline*): I haven't been for five years. There's a group of us.
TE (*still not looking up*): Well, you're not going.
You: Well … I … I … Am. (*Yay!*)
TE (*standing up, fixing you with glacial stare*): No. You're not. I'll tell you why. You won't be here Saturday.

You: Whaaat?
TE (*throwing down a sheaf of documents*): Read them.
You (*glancing at divorce papers*): What are ...?
TE: I've had enough. You're pathetic, spineless, a wimp.
You: But ...
TE: Oh, shut up. It's like being married to a poodle. I'm off.

What she says

'No, he won't.'
'No, he doesn't.'
'No, he can't.'

What you need to do

When you're on your American fly-drive, make a detour. Drop her off in Compton, LA. See how her misandry goes down with the local gangs.

Learn some Giant Haystacks moves. Every time she makes a verbal lunge at you, just sit on her.

Get down to Whips'R'Us, truss yourself up in some top-of-the-range dominatrix gear, and stride into the bedroom, announcing, 'Who's the daddy now?'

Chapter Three
Bosses/Colleagues

Beelzeboss

What she does

What *doesn't* she?

But let's start at the very beginning. All you know is that she's your line manager and you've just landed the promotion of your career. No wonder you're dancing to *Hi Ho Silver Lining* at your predecessor's leaving do. You don't stop to think, 'Why is she off? when she hasn't got another job to go to?' or wonder why she keeps casting ominous glances your way, or why she's on her ninth beaker of punch. And *she* ain't dancing.

But the most troubling omen of all occurs in the Ladies' Loo (otherwise known as the crying room).

You're washing your hands. The light flickers and fizzes. The sound of dripping water echoes and *Hi Ho Silver Lining* fades away. Predecessor grips your arm and thrusts something in your hand. 'Aim for the light!' And then she's gone. You unclasp your palm – nestling in it is a tiny silver angel.

You shrug it off. Let's get down to business. BB summons you to a 'getting to know you' session over lunch. 'What makes you tick?' she smiles benignly. Sub-text:

'What's your Achilles heel? Because I'm going to be exploiting that for the next six years.'

So you tell her. Well done! Now she holds the key to your destruction.

Solitary lamp illuminating your desk, you beavering away at large document. BB appears in your peripheral vision.

You: Oh! Err, I've done the report. Did you want it now? Hope it covers all the options ... I've devoted a section to each separate client ... and then I summed up ...

BB (*interrupting*): Yes, yes, hand it here. I'll look at it later.

Five minutes before you leave the office.

BB: Could you come in, please. Sit down. What I've done is make a few corrections.

You: (*A few? It's a massacre.*)

BB: If you look at them, you'll see the way we work here.

You: (*I know the way we work here. Don't I?*)

BB: What you need to do is go away and have a look at it again. Take on board my comments and bring me something I can work with.

You: Right ... when do you ...?

BB: Not urgent. Take it home, look at it again tonight. Tomorrow's meeting will be fine.

You: The breakfast meeting?

BB: Yes. But don't work through the night on it. Ha ha.

You: (*Does that chemist downstairs do caffeine tablets, travel pillows and disposable knickers?*)

Five months on, you're starting to look like Al Pacino in *Insomnia*. Your workload would make Sisyphus think 'Blimey, there's always someone worse off than me.'

Even if you do manage to get to the bottom of the in-tray, and you're just about to tick off your five-foot-long list of 'things to do', she'll be back with the previous six months' work, littered with Post-it notes outlining her amendments, clarifications, quibbles, niggles and sticking points. And oh, by the way, your personality isn't commensurate with the company's policy.

She would find fault with a foetus. You start checking the staff directory to make sure you haven't been moved to a different department. Called Purgatory. Your viewing choices are now erring on the satanic side: Friday: *The Devil Rides Out*. Saturday: *The Devil's Advocate*. Sunday. *The Devil Wears Prada*. (But you had to take that back. There wasn't any goat-slaughtering in it.)

You don't just take your work home with you: her demonic features accompany you on the bus, into your home, are present at supper, behind you in the bathroom mirror, join you in your bedroom, surface in your waking thoughts, your sleeping thoughts and any thoughts in between. You're possessed! 'How's the job going?' someone asks you innocently at a dinner party. 'Evil is abroad,' you shriek, wild-eyed.

You, head down at desk, 45 phials of Rescue Remedy flanking your computer. BB appears in your peripheral vision.

BB: It's good to have you back. All better now up there? (*Tapping your forehead*)
You: Still a bit ... erm ... shaky.
BB: They give you drugs for that, though, don't they?
You: Yeah ... I think they're doing the trick. Just got to avoid ... (*Voice dropping to a hoarse whisper*) stress.
BB: Right, back to work. Got just the thing to ease you in again. I want you to be the keynote speaker at the Directors' Conference.
You: (*Gulp.*)
BB: Don't worry. You can take your pills up to the podium.

Later, at conference. You, perspiring, pulse racing, trying hard to picture dolphins in a tranquil sea.

You: ... in summary, the cohesion of the company depends on strong inter-departmental liaison and clear communication at all levels. Any questions? No, okay, good. Thank you.
BB (*raising hand*): I'd like to make a couple of points on your presentation.

Beelzeboss

You (*where are the dolphins, where are the dolphins?*): Ermmmm ...

BB: It might just be me, but some of that was hazy. And muddled ... Could you not have used PowerPoint?

You: Well, being off, I didn't really get time to organise ...

BB (*turning to MD, muttering*): She's not been well.

You: It was ... just ...

BB: We're all very understanding here about people with mental health issues.

You: I'm ... not ... mental ...

BB: Right. Now, I just want to go over that point you made halfway through.

You (*rummaging through papers*): I can't quite find ... I don't know ... sorry, what page ...?

BB: That's okay. We'll wait.

You (*scattering paper everywhere, knocking lectern over, spilling water down blouse*): It's here ... *somewhere* ... (*Sobbing now and on hands and knees*) I'm not supposed to be *UNDER ANY PRESSURE!*

BB (*approaching lectern, bending down as if to proffer help. Slides Post-it under your eyeline, depicting a matchstick figure tumbling over a cliff, and hisses*): That's your career. (*Stands up, turning to directors*) Right. Lunch at the Fallen Angel anyone?

What she says

Nothing. She's sent you to Coventry.

What you need to do

Get hold of a Catholic priest fast. Preferably one that still does exorcisms.

Work to Ruler

What he does

Bullies upwards. You're his boss, but he's the despot. He might not have the power, the status and the salary you have, but he's calling all the shots. How does he manage that then? Simple. He snorts at your suggestions, scoffs at your ideas, snipes at your proposals, slates your vision and sneers at your hair.

Unlike the SS, he just won't take orders, and his contempt for you knows no bounds. Favourite weapons include ignoring you, sniggering with an embarrassed colleague at the back of the room while you're presenting the annual team-building seminar, and keeping you waiting ... All The Time.

You, periodically looking through glass partition towards WtR's desk, decisively reaching for phone, picking it up, putting it down again, picking it up, putting it down again, before, finally, picking it up and pressing WtR's extension rapidly.

You: Can you just come into my office for a minute?

WtR replaces receiver and carries on working, i.e., reading his personal emails and playing Mahjong.

You (*popping head out of office*): Are you free? Can I see you now?

WtR sighs emphatically.

You (*stepping out of office*): Are you coming?
WtR: What's it about?
You (*walking over to his desk*): I've had some thoughts about the meeting yesterday, just wondering if ... you ... could ...

WtR's phone rings.

You: Leave it for voice mail, please.
WtR (*picking up receiver*): Alright mate? Yeah, expect so, hold on a minute. (*Puts hand over receiver, looks up at you*) Are we done?
You: I'll try you again when you're not so busy. (*Retreating to office*)

He's this bad? So sack him, except you can't because he knows his contract to every last paragraph, sub-clause and comma. If there's the slightest danger he might have to make a little extra effort to meet a deadline, he will quote section 15.1.6. 2ii, which refers to practices last encountered during the Corn Laws.

He's Peter Sellers playing Fred Kite in *I'm All Right Jack* – except he's in a union of one. He would make the job of road-testing the latest sports car, while simultaneously being fondled by a nubile blonde, seem like a trial.

He's not hot on verbal communication but more than makes up for it with muttering, tutting and rolling his eyes – and that's just if you ask him to open the window. He spends so much time on the phone to Human Resources checking his terms of employment that they've got a dedicated team of two just to answer his calls.

Eventually you have to remind yourself, with the help of that sign on the door that says 'Boss', that you are actually his superior because a) you're photocopying 250 brochures for the presentation as you 'don't want to bother him', b) taking his calls and telling people 'he's in a meeting', and c) doing his dry-cleaning run.

You, nervously approaching WtR at his desk.

You: Got a good little number for you tomorrow.
WtR (*exuding air of utter boredom*): Really?
You: Yes, that corporate do at Wentworth. I can't make it as head office is coming down.
WtR: And ...?
You: We ... ll. It's free champagne, four-course meal, your wife can go along too, all you have to do is meet and greet, sit at the same table and enjoy yourself.

Work to Ruler 75

WtR (*letting out a big sigh, while shaking head*): Nap, nap, nope, nap, naap, nope ...

You: You can't make it?

WtR: Nap, naap, nope, nah, nap.

You: So, what's the problem?

WtR: Evening do, is it?

You: Yes, but a car will pick you up and take you home. Nice little jolly.

WtR: Nahp. Nope. (*Reaches into drawer, pulls out contract*) Outside working hours, isn't it?

You: Well, yes, but it's not really work.

WtR: I would be there as an employee of this company.

You: Just go along and have a good time.

WtR: Overtime then?

You: Well, to be honest, with the car, the champagne, the meal and everything ...

WtR: So, no overtime?

You: Mmmm ... no.

WtR: No. Can. Do.

You: Ah, thing is they do actually want one of us there ...

WtR looks up and shrugs.

You (*to yourself*): Okay, let's have a think ... all I need to do then is reschedule head office for next week. Trouble is that's the start of my holiday in Cornwall, but that's okay, I could always tell the kids we'll do Disneyland at Christmas. (*Turning back to him*) Right, that's sorted then.

What he says

'Before we do anything, I'll have a sausage and bacon bap on white, plenty of butter, two tomato sauce sachets, black coffee, two sugars, don't stir it, and a Twix. Bring me back the change.'

'See ya.' (As the clock flashes 5hrs 30minutes. 000000 seconds.)

'Siiiiiiiighhhhhhhhhhhiiiiiiiiiiiiiiiiiigggghhhhhhhhhhh hiiiiiiiiiiiiiiiiigggggghhhhhhhhhhhhhhhhhhhhhhhhhhhhh-hhhh.'

What you need to do

Get hold of a road sign – you're the boss, steal one if you have to – that reads 'Danger! Massive Obstruction!' and put it on his desk.

Put him forward for a promotion working for your opposite number at head office – Beelzeboss (see above).

Organise a works outing. Don't tell him it's just him and he's off on a jaunt to the Dnepropetrovsk Gulag.

Big Rancour

What he does

Takes bitterness to the *n*th degree. He's had his day – and it didn't end with a dreamy sunset, a beautiful wife and a Porsche. So now he has a new ambition: to screw up *your* career. Because he can. Usually to be found in a glass-walled sub-section of the main office, where he can keep an eye on his underlings, and plot their downfalls, one by one. To say he finds young, enthusiastic subordinates a threat is like saying Jack the Ripper had intimacy issues.

Sooner or later, he will spew his bile on you. Don't ever relax, even when you think he's focussing all his energies on sending your colleagues to an early grave marked 'work-related stress'. He has not forgotten about you – you're just in the folder marked 'Future Projects'.

They've barely stretchered out the last of his casualties, before he's targeting his next victim: you. You won't even have time to scramble up the stairs to Human Resources. They won't help you anyway. They know the best way to deal with BR is to keep him in his side(-lined) office, where he can't balls up the real business of the company. You, as you will soon discover, are expendable.

If you're still reckless enough to shine at your job, you

may as well take yourself off to the stationery cupboard, get a sheet of Basildon Bond and write your own letter of dismissal. It'll save him the effort.

You, standing right in front of BR's desk. Five minutes pass. You move slightly closer. Two minutes pass. You shuffle forward an inch. One minute passes. You are now so close you can smell his Nescafé breath. BR continues staring at computer.

You (*suddenly*): I'm handing in my notice.

BR stares at computer, doesn't answer.

You: I've been headhunted.

BR stares at computer, doesn't answer.

You: I'm going to be leaving ... soon ...

BR remains staring at computer, not answering.

You: It's a new company in Birmingham. They want me to start in a couple of weeks' time.

BR stares at computer, doesn't answer.

You: Apparently, they saw the proposal I did for Wilson and Picketts ...

BR rummaging in pockets, rattling loose change.

You: They've recently merged, and they want me to head up their communications division.

BR pops a Polo.

You: There'll be a team of 25 beneath me. I'll be in charge.
BR: Who's daft enough to take you?

You, opening mouth, shutting it, opening it again.

BR: What are you going to be? MD of the scouts' Bob a Job week?
You: It's actually a really good chance to take my career to the next level.

BR makes sound like a small balloon deflating.

You: ... there might even be the opportunity to work abroad, they've got offices in Dubai and Melbourne. It's a brilliant opportunity. It is!
BR (*leaning back, plonking feet on desk*): Birmingham?
You: Yes?
BR: Shit town, shit football team.

What he says

'Don't get too excited. You were the only candidate.'
'What was that university you said you went to? University of Teletubbies?'

'Those awards? They just pick the winner out of a hat.'

What you need to do

Cultivate a shambolic appearance and weep freely as you proclaim that you 'can't cope'. He'll assume he's got you on a never-ending stint of 'gardening leave' already and move on to the next victim. Leaving you time to plan your exit with your wits intact.

Keep your sanity by messing with his mind. When he's giving you a volcanic dressing-down about a spelling mistake, agree that, yes, indeed, you are a 'lazy, inept, going-nowhere loser'. And watch as he tries to figure out what game *you* might be playing.

Suck up for England: every bully needs a henchman, and you could be the Hermann to his Adolf. (Although morally reprehensible, you will avoid being in the firing line.)

Poacher-turned-Gamekeeper

What she does

Makes childless women cry. She was once the ball-breaking daughter of Margaret Thatcher. But that was before she became a mum. Now she's a hybrid of Nigella Lawson, the Madonna and Ma Walton. Incredible! She's the first woman on the planet to have a baby.

But this isn't ordinary mother's pride; this is power, status and one-upmanship. And she's never prouder than when she's thrusting it in barren women's faces.

A scrum of squawking females, clogging up an office walkway. At its centre, PtG 'wearing' her baby in a raffia and muslin over-the-shoulder, round-the-waist (twice) swaddling papoose sling.

You: How was it then? (*Make it quick*)
PtG: Well, (*off I go!*) extraordinary. I've never known pain like it, but it was good pain ... the midwife said she'd never seen anyone so brave ... I'd already stated in the birth plan that I wasn't to be given any drugs ... and because I'd been massaging my perineum with sweet almond oil, I only tore slightly and didn't have to be cut ... I just held on to my doula and screamed ... I didn't care, the language was awful, the doctors were in hysterics ... but I just had gas and

air and refused the epidural ... they couldn't believe I could go that long without pain relief ... but then, I didn't want to be doped out on pethidine ... I've already started on the pelvic floor exercises, God, my partner wouldn't like me flapping about down there, or he might change his mind about having another one ... and I've already given little one a good dose of milk, he latched on beautifully of course first time I got him to the breast, and it felt almost orgasmic ... apparently, my breasts are the best type for feeding, and my milk is like gold top, he can't get enough of it ...

You (*glancing at her feet, in hospital slippers*): Have they discharged you yet?

Just like the reformed smoker who can't be within yards of ash, the PtG has no time now for the arid and fallow, even though she spent her entire adult life till now spitting vitriol at the very notion having children might be fulfilling. She has now rapidly reinvented herself as the Mother of all Mothers. She was either lying then, or she's lying now.

Back then, she would gleefully freeze out any woman returning from maternity leave and remark loudly that her brain had 'gone to mush'. Now she's a mother (i.e., she had sex and did what any 15-year-old could do), she's got the monopoly on selflessness.

So your brother's dodging bullets in Sudan while treating AIDS orphans? Big deal. Until you've had to postpone a spa weekend because your baby developed a temperature of 105 degrees, you don't know the meaning of self-sacrifice.

In fact, you don't know the meaning of anything. Let's face it, you don't have any children. Your life's meaningless.

You, sitting in front of computer. Suddenly, voices off, 'Oooh, here he is again', 'He's grown since yesterday, hasn't he? Aaaaw, he's so sweet!', 'Bless him', 'Aaaw', 'Oooh, can I have a go, give him to me', 'Couldn't you just eat him?' You sigh and huddle down behind screen.

PtG (*plonking car seat, complete with mewling babe, on your desk*): Hiya! How's it going? Oooh, work, eh? You poor thing!

You: Fine. (*Pause*) Is he ... is he ... teethi ...?

PtG: You'll never guess what he can do now. Come here, no come here, right, you do this, I'll hold him here, look, look! Look what he's doing! Isn't that brilliant!!

You: Mmmm ... aaah ...

PtG: This morning we were getting ready to come here and you'll never guess ...

You: Won't I?

PtG: He looked straight into my eyes and did the biggest, most beautiful smile I've ever seen on a child ever. It was the most amazing thing that's ever happened to me – and ever will.

You: Good. Good.

PtG: I can't explain it. I think until you've had children yourself, you just can't imagine how they're going to change your life in such a fantastic way. It's as if he's been here forever.

You: Mmmm hmmm.

PtG: Anyway, how are you? How's the IVF, I forgot about that. Weren't you on your final cycle?

You (*quietly*): Yeah.

PtG: Did it work?

You (*even quieter*): No.

PtG: Oh. Anyway, got to go, we're doing baby Mozart. (*Walks away, then suddenly turns back towards desk*) What am I like? Nearly forgot him!

Try to have a conversation with her that doesn't include the following phrases: organic baby food, Montessori schools, breastfeeding in public, flash cards, Muzzy language DVDs, baby signing. It won't happen.

She's only got one thing on her mind these days. And that's rubbing everyone's face in her fecundity.

What she says

'Why would anybody want to have some squawking, puking, red-faced creature that costs you a fortune?' (Before Baby.)

'I feel so sorry for those women who will never know the transcendental wonder of bringing a new soul into Gaia.' (After Baby.)

What you need to do

Ask her why she came back to work full-time, if being a mother is so wonderful and fulfilling and all.

Change the holiday rota so she has to work every Easter, Christmas, half-term, Whitsun, May Day and every single, last inset day.

Wait a few years for advances in genetic science. Then have a designer baby that's prettier, cleverer, taller – and pees all over hers. Literally.

The PG Chimp

What he does

Makes like a monkey. Incompetence doesn't come close. This is like discovering a chimp has escaped from the zoo, landed in the boss's chair, and is causing havoc, smashing up projects and smearing all your hard work with his grubby, ham-fisted paws.

This is a man who has somehow landed himself a Premier-League job. His 'abilities', however, mean he should be languishing in a non-division hinterland. He behaves as if he's got the workload of one Egyptian ordered to build single-handedly the entire Valley of the Kings. Or the equivalent of God creating the Universe (in five days).

See him, that Italian-suited, file-carrying, iPhone-clasping whirl of activity, blowing through the office like a half-baked hurricane in Harlesden? He's busy, busy, busy, isn't he? Yep. Busy doing nothing. If he stopped updating you every two minutes on 'another bloody email I could do without', he could have got through a week's work.

The word 'meeting', of course, is enough to make him wet his pants with excitement. They are his lifeblood and he will happily spend all day in one. (Gets round the awkward business of work.) His PA will be ordered to stockpile

Jammy Dodgers, ham sandwiches, bananas (*quelle surprise*), flasks of tea, nibbles, mineral water – sparkling and still – and pyjamas.

First item on the agenda is the content of the sandwiches. Then the main business of the meeting is to establish who is doing what, what is being done, how much has been done and 'where we are at'. This takes three hours of your day. Brilliant. Three hours discussing the work that you could've completed in the time it took to talk about the work you need to complete.

Perhaps he's just an annoying buffoon? Wrong. Because deep down in his shrivelled little soul a tiny glimmer of self-awareness flickers, and he knows he's not up to the job. *I've screwed up. But I'm not taking the rap. They can*. So he blames the chimps' tea party mayhem on you.

PGC, plonking his backside on corner of your desk, displacing a year's worth of ordered data across the carpet tiles.

PGC: Done it yet?
You: Not quite sure exactly what it was that you were wanting me to do ...
PGC: Just Google people ... you know, you'll find a lot of them on the internet ... (*Picking up first page of your business degree thesis*) Check the websites ... ring around ... (*Looking

at page) Try my Rolodex ... have a look in the file from last year, but obviously we want something different from that ... (*Scrunches up page*) Edgier ... more upfront ... cutting edge ... (*Lobs paper into far corner of office*) I'll need that by two for the meeting.

You (*none the wiser*): Do you want me to find examples from our competitors from the internet. (*What the eff do you want!?*)

PGC (*sighing*): No. We need to look at things a different way ...

You (*completely baffled*): Right, so should I see what they've done and come up with a few ideas of where we can be completely original?

PGC: Do the thing I asked you to do.

You (*sliding into catalepsy*): Errrrrr ...

PGC: And get it printed out by two and put a copy in for upstairs. And don't forget to send duplicates to the directors' list. (*Walks away triumphantly*)

You (*turning to everyone in office, hands outstretched imploringly*): Anybody?

Followed by the 2 p.m. meeting in the boardroom. PGC, sitting at a higher chair than everyone else, flanked by his area managers. You, standing at the end of a 50-metre-long, highly polished table.

PGC: Let's get started. Have you got those figures I asked for?

You (*No! What figures?*): The figures for ...?

PGC: The figures.

You (*panicking, 'You're not helping me here'*): Do you mean the ... comparisons with the other companies?

PGC: No. I mean the figures. (*Looking at cohorts as if to say, 'Look what I have to put up with'*)

You: What I've actually drawn up is a summary of proposals that will make us original and cutting edge within our own budget, which is what I think was the gist of what you'd asked me to do ...

PGC: I didn't ask you to do that.

You (*Didn't you? Damn, what's my name? adding quietly*): That's what I've done.

PGC: (*to others*): Sorry, everyone. It appears you've all had a wasted journey. Apparently *someone* hasn't provided the figures you asked for.

You: Excuse me, I'm sorry, you genuinely didn't ask me to get any figures. I would have remembered that.

Slight pause as cohorts look to PGC.

PGC: And another thing ... I ... I don't expect (*raising voice*) to walk by your desk and (*waving finger furiously*) see your (*clenching fist*) coat on the back of your chair when there are (*slamming fist on table*) PERFECTLY GOOD PEGS!

After several months of this primate pickaxing away at the seam of your self-confidence, you will be calling your local recruitment office to see if they have any openings in basket weaving.

What he says

'Do I have to spell it out?' (Yes, you do actually.)

'What is it you don't understand about what I've just explained?' (All of it.)

'Have a banana.'

What you need to do

Quick, call the local zoo! Tell them to bring a large net.

Automatically do the opposite of what you think he's asked you to do. You've got as much chance of it being right.

Get yourself assigned to a 'special project'. (Office speak for a nice long bed rest with Classic FM in the background.)

Chapter Four

Family

The Remote Controller

What he does

Runs his family like he runs his office, and if he could sack the lot of you he would, because quite frankly, you're just not up to the job.

Your free will was signed away at the moment of conception. Not for you blissful idle childhood days scrumping for apples, playing Poohsticks and daydreaming in the tree house. Slacker! Every second spent not sleeping or on the toilet must have a purpose – his purpose.

On your eighth birthday he presents you with a beautiful leather-bound diary and tells you to make sure you fill something in every day. 'Thanks Dad!' No. He means it. It's not a diary, it's a time and motion study.

Any notions you might have about following your own path, marching to your own beat, cutting your own cloth, forget all that – if it doesn't have his rubber stamp of approval, it ain't happening.

That's why you may get a Talking Heads moment in your 30s, freeze mid-riveting a warship, and think, 'How did I get here? I wanted to be a phlebotomist.'

Did he come up with the blueprint for CCTV (the talking one that tells you off if you wear your sweatshirt with the hood up)? Because he's been running your life since day one. Your wishes are *his* commands. 'What about *my* feelings/opinions/beliefs/views?' you periodically cry. His reply is always the same: 'And ...?'

The bell-shaped conservatory of your parents' house. Family gathered around a glass-topped raffia coffee table, your kids sulking because Grandad doesn't have a Wii, you and your mum seated either side of RC, like handmaidens, your husband attempting to perch one cheek on the Economy 7 heater.

RC: Right, nearly halfway through February. Time to get this sorted.

All raise eyes heavenward.

You (*muttering*): It gets earlier every year.
RC: Diaries out. From the top. 23rd July to 30th July – children with us. You to deliver, you to pick up. 7th August Stansted, Gate 5. Priority seating for me and your mother. Toulouse, then overnight stop at Bagnères-de-Bigorre. Aim to reach foothills mid-morning.
You (*tentatively*): Foothills of ... what ... what are we going to do then?
RC: You and ... (*pointing at your partner*) you'll need all-weather gear and proper shoes. And I *mean* proper shoes.

You: What ... what are we ...?
RC: There's going to be a lot of walking. It's all walking.
You: So you'll be gone most of the day?
RC: *We'll all* be gone most of the day.
You: Don't know if the boys will manage ...
RC: They'll have to. We're booked into a different place every night. If they don't make it, they don't get fed and they don't get bed.
You: Okay. Well, I think we're going to have to ... (*glancing at partner, who nods*) make our own way ... or stay in a gîte ...
RC: You don't *look* at the Pyrenees. You walk them.
You (*quietly*): They're three and five years old.
RC (*head down, silently jotting on piece of paper, which he then holds up directly in front of you*): Here are three reasons why you're going to go. Read them. Out loud.
You (*reading*): 'I've researched it. I've booked it. I've paid for it.'

When you still lived under his roof, you were just too plain frit to argue back. Now you're all grown up, you still don't do it. Because he's got a new weapon: his heart. (Has he got one?) You might try a little quiet reasoning (see above), but any further resistance is futile. You'll be met with this: 'Are you *deliberately* trying to give me a heart attack?'

You're not Daddy's Girl – You're Daddy's Dogsbody.

What he says

'No.'
'No.'
'No.'

What you need to do

Volunteer you and your family on a witness protection programme. (Minor detail: you *will* have to hang with bigtime drug dealers for ten years, gaining their trust by becoming a mule, transporting 500kg of cocaine up your jacksie from Bolivia to Rotterdam, then handing over the haul in a brown paper bag by foggy moonlight to DI Bent of the Yard under Hungerford Bridge.)

Wicked Whittler

What she does

Puts you down. That's it. That's her childrearing technique in a nutshell. Did she read the book *How to Screw up Your Kids for Life*, instead of Dr Spock? No, she wrote it. Her favoured chapters: 'Knock their Confidence for Six'; 'Anorexia/Bulimia, Which is Best for Baby?'; 'How to Rear a Social Misfit'.

Were you born from the womb or in a petrie dish? Because you seem to be the subject of an experiment she's conducting in how to create the world's most miserable adult.

Never mind that you're a solicitor, your partner has his own business, you've gone up another rung on the property ladder, you've just come back from two weeks in Miami, if your self-esteem was any lower, you'd be excavating it from the core of the earth.

Because wherever you go, whatever you do, there's an evil Jiminy Cricket sitting on your shoulder, jabbering in your ear, whittling away at your self-esteem. 'You haven't/ you couldn't/ you mustn't/ you won't be/ you can't/you shouldn't/ you don't/ YOU'LL NEVER.'

Wicked Whittler

The voice is strangely familiar. It should be. It's your own dear mum's.

You learned to walk at six months. You had to; it was the only way you were going to get your bottle. You taught yourself first aid at the age of six. You had to; she didn't do, 'There, there, let mummy kiss it better.' They gave you a Most Likely to Succeed Trophy at school. She told you to take it back. And reported you to the head for theft. You ran the London Marathon. She said: 'Paula Radcliffe did it in 2 hours 15 minutes. Way ahead of you.'

And you're still wondering why you and your therapist have just celebrated your 20th anniversary? Here are some clues.

You: Mummy, look – I drew a cat and a flower for you.
WW: Which is which?

You: Is this okay for the school disco?
WW: Yes, if you want to look like a prostitute.

You: I've been invited to dinner with the neighbours.
WW: Do they know how much you put away?

You: Mum, he's left me.
WW: I'm not surprised.

You: I'd love a baby.
WW: Let's hope it doesn't have your chin.

You: I've just won the Nobel Prize for Peace.
WW: They'll be giving it to Robert Mugabe next.

Bloody hell, you've been reared by Joan Crawford. She never misses an opportunity to denigrate. Her opening gambit when introducing you to people may as well be, 'Have you met my daughter? She's rubbish.'

She's elbowing your enemies out of the way to have the privilege of being the first to tell you you've got fat, you're getting jowly and you've developed a ten-to-two walk. But look in the mirror. It doesn't crack, you're an attractive woman. To WW, though, you might as well be a bulldog wearing lipstick, Gordon Ramsay in a backless chiffon frock, Andrew Lloyd Webber in a basque and stockings.

A more appropriate subject for her maternal instincts would be a tank of stick insects. And age will not mellow her, even when she's rattling out her last breath, infirm, incontinent and incomprehensible. Don't expect a death-bed reconciliation.

You, on hands and knees, under bed, with J-cloth and anti-bacterial fluids. A gurgling ensues from above.

You: I'm here, Mum.
WW: Ga ga ga ga ga ga ga ga ...
You: Can you hear me?
WW: Ga ga ga ga ga ga ga ...
You: I'm right by your side.

WW raises herself on one elbow, beckoning you closer.

You: What are you trying to say?
WW (*croaking*): DAMN YOU TO HELL! (*Expires*)

What she says

'Your problem is you think the world owes you a living. You haven't got the backbone to cope in the real world. You've always been a drifter. You've got no staying power. You make a mess of everything, You never see a job through. You think everything's going to be handed to you on a plate. When are you going to grow up? Will you just STOP ROCKING YOUR HIGHCHAIR!'

What you need to do

Tell her you've booked her on a skiing trip at the world's newest resort; The Hindu Kush.

Next time she asks you if you've sorted out the granny annexe, tell her there's no need as she's booked into the

Rainbow's End Seniors Complex (motto: 'The only way you're leaving here is in a box!')

Put her greatest skill to practical use – give her a hunk of wood and a sharp knife. It's a lot more constructive than carving pieces out of you.

Me-Me Mum

What she does

Her own thing. Need help with the kids, moving house, or sorting out your finances? You won't get it from MMM. She'll be on a cookery course in Spain, a sailing trip in the Maldives or channelling her Iroquois spirit guide. You'll regularly have to remind her of your name. Nothing to do with dementia, she's just utterly self-absorbed.

She's been rooting for herself ever since you can remember, and after your dad came to his senses and baled out, she took the opportunity to take a big old dip in 'Lake Me'. Her religion is self-worship. Any thought for the needs and wants of others (i.e., her children) is heresy.

She had to do the children thing, of course, but being a mother wasted an awful lot of time which she would rather have spent on 'Project Me'. You were an encumbrance for far too long. Once you reached the age of consent, she dumped you for someone better. Herself.

Pointless ringing her to tell her about your miscarriage. She's got to get off to her yogalates class. Don't bother popping in for a chat about your failing marriage. She's immersed in *Be as Selfish as You Like*, by Dr Sickman Fraud. And don't even think about telling her you've lost your job.

Me-Me Mum

She's too busy with her own 'work': boob jobs, dye jobs, teeth jobs, nose jobs, thigh jobs and blow jobs.

Ah, that's the other thing: she's got her second wind, and God help you. Ever since she read that 60 is the new sexy, she's been shoving it in your face. Now it's ME time and that means MY wants, MY needs, MY desires and, oh dear, MY newfound appetite for sex.

Her selfishness knows no bounds. It's a global enterprise – the world is there purely for her to plunder as she searches for the meaning of life. (So long as it's just hers.)

She'll be taking long-haul holidays trying to find herself. (*Found yourself yet? No? Still looking. Okay.*) And, while she's there, she might as well try to jump the bones of the poor indigenous populations. Never mind Italian waiters; she's into Inuit, Masai warriors, sherpa guides, aborigines and pygmies.

She may be gone for some time. Probably long enough and frequent enough to miss the family's entire roll-call of births, deaths and marriages.

You, amidst a sea of tulle, gypsophila, rice paper, rose petals and sushi parcels, punching in MMM's speed dial. Eventually, MMM picks up.

You: Hi, Mum. Just to let you know, the vicar is fine about

moving the date to the one you suggested and we've printed out the new invitations and they've gone out. So there's no problem.

MMM: Hmmmm.

You (*suspiciously*): What?

MMM: I'm not going to be able to make it now.

You: WHAT!?

MMM: It's only two days before I fly out to Rajasthan.

You: Since when have you been going to Rajasthan?

MMM: What it is, I've found this fantastic tiger haven. A group of us will be led out and we can actually get close enough to ...

You (*angry*): ... get eaten?

MMM: ... we're staying in a former palace, run by – get this – a lovely Asian man, who was educated at Shrewsbury. So, what I need ...

You: Right. But you could still make it. The wedding's Saturday and you're flying out on the Monday? What's the problem?

MMM (*dismissively*): I need to sleep. And pack. I'm not just going on a day trip to Blackpool. I have to prepare myself spiritually. I want to be totally energised when I set off.

You: Okay. Don't bother with the evening do. You can leave early, sleep till whenever Sunday. You could start packing now. That still leaves you loads of time ...

MMM: I am *not* knocking myself out to get to *your* wedding and then have *my* first India experience ruined.

You: Mum, we changed the date to suit YOU.
MMM: And now it doesn't suit me.

What she says

'It's not selfishness. It's putting my needs first.' (At all times.)

'I'm exploring myself.' (You can only pray she does this in the privacy of her own home.)

'Have you met Efuk? I brought him back from Bodrum.'

What you need to do

Anything you want – crack addiction, whoring, arson, arms-dealing - she won't notice.

Doesn't matter how old you are. Put an ad in your local paper looking for an adoptive mum, explaining yours has disappeared up her own fundament.

Pen your own self-help book, the one you've entitled *Get Over Yourself, You Selfish Cow*, and present it to her on her birthday.

The Toxin-Law

What she does

Eats away at your family from the inside. You think the Ebola virus is destructive? Meet the poisonous pathogen more commonly known as your sister-in-law.

Remember that sun-dappled afternoon when your brother announced he was bringing his new girlfriend around for Sunday lunch? Mum's in the kitchen with floury hands, Dad's uncorking the wine, you're at the mullioned window with your siblings and assorted spouses, excitedly anticipating their arrival. Hark! Even *Family Favourites* is on the radiogram.

Suddenly, there's a mysterious icy blast. The peace lily shrivels in its pot. A dark shadow is cast across the Wilton at Rosedean. She's here. Later, the potatoes are plated up, the chicken is carved, glasses chink. All's well. Savour that moment. For verily, there is a plague on your house.

Her marriage to your brother is the culmination of a sophisticated brainwashing operation. She reprogrammes him against your family quicker than you can say 'Waco'. Not so much his wife, more of a control-freaking succubus.

You won't notice the effects of initial exposure, but gradually the infection takes hold.

Bullies, Bitches and Bastards

Six months later. The Cosy Barn's banquet suite. A swing band in full swing. Singing, laughing, dancing, chattering, gay bantering abounding. TL sitting alone, watching. You approach her, bearing a tray.

You: Can I get you a vol-au-vent?
TL: I won't, thanks. The last one tasted a bit off.
You: Oh. Satay stick? Bhajee? Mini pizza?
TL: Oh, no. Don't fancy any of that. So how long did it take your mum to do all this?
You: Oh, we all helped.
TL: God, 40 years. That's amazing, isn't it?
You: I know, it gives you hope, doesn't it?
TL: Because they're chalk and cheese, really.
You: Weellll ... I suppose so.
TL: Your dad's very outgoing. Your mum's more of a homebod.
You: Well, Mum is more of an old-fashioned housewife.
TL: Whereas you're a real career girl. Is she still on at you to settle down?
You: Yeah, it's a pain.
TL: Mmmmm ... I bet.
You: Yeah, sometimes you think, 'change the record, Mum'. Just because I want to do something different with my life.
TL: Mmmmmm ...
You (*conspiratorially*): To tell you the truth, it's really been get-

The Toxin-Law

ting on my nerves lately because she keeps on at me about getting married.
TL: Well, it's your life. Tell her to stick it.
You: Do you know what? I might just do that.

TL laughs and walks away. Job done. You, inexplicably nauseated. And it's not the vol-au-vents.

Great. You're now character-assassinating your mum on her 40th wedding anniversary. Gradually, the spores multiply – your heretofore placid parents and serene siblings are bickering, cussing and squabbling like never before. Meanwhile, the agent of antagonism is standing coolly in the corner, looking on. Nothing to do with her. What are they *like*, your family? Well, they weren't like this before TL fetched up at Rosedean.

Hotfoot from her own sociopathic brood of shysters, shirkers and shafters, she's certainly not having any of your 'happy families' malarkey. You're all far too close for her liking. There's work to do – splitting you all asunder.

You, your husband, your brother, your sisters, their husbands, your mother, your father, your uncle, your aunt, your cousins, your great-aunt, your grandmother, your one-month-old baby gathered under a towering pine tree, singing The Holly and the Ivy. *TL flicking through magazine in corner.*

You (*finishing on a high note*): ... the holly bears the crooo-ooo-ooownnn ... ah ... lovely. Right, everyone, I'll just get on with basting the goose. (*Turning to TL*) Fancy a sherry?

TL: God, no. Have you got any paracetamol?

You: You not feeling well?

TL: No. Got a blinding headache. *That* isn't helping (*Eyes swivelling towards 92-year-old Grandma singing-along-a Val Doonican*)

You: Oh well, it's only once a year. (*Going into kitchen, sticking Vs up at her behind closed door before returning with paracetamol and a glass of water*)

TL (*glaring at your newborn in Moses basket, who is beginning to grizzle. Shudders*): That goes *right* through me. (*Swallows pills. Walks towards kitchen and, in passing, picks up basket and moves it to far corner of room*) That's better.

You (*aghast, running headlong towards baby, who is now at full wail, plucking him from the basket and cleaving him fast unto your heart before running full tilt into kitchen, followed by your mother. You slam door shut*): ... Did you *see* that? Did you see what she did?! Picked him up like a bag of ... bloody *shopping* and dumped him in the corner, right by the window in a draught – in a DRAUGHT! ... That is it ... I've had enough of her ... She's going ... No Mum, don't, get off me, I'm not having her in my house a minute longer ... Yes, I know it's Christmas Day, does she?! ...(*Husband scuttles into kitchen*) Where were you?! You tw ... Didn't you, didn't you see that? What do you mean, 'no'?! She did it right in front of you. What were you doing? You were in there ... why didn't you stop her? ... Oh, I know, too bloody busy fiddling with batteries ... Don't you tell me to calm down ... Don't patronise me ... Don't you DARE defend her. You're the one that calls her Toxin-Law. (*Dad slopes in next*) No, Dad, just leave it, LEAVE IT! ... I'll tell you what she's done now ... Yes, actually it does matter what she's done, yes, Mum, you're right ... Yes, listen to Mum, you *have* let her walk all over us as a family ... (*Sisters, cousins etc. filing in with 'What's going on?' 'What's happening?' 'Why's everyone getting so heated?'*) ... I just want to know why didn't you stop her moving your son ... Why's it always me? I bet if I hadn't gone upstairs the other day, he'd have been over the balcony ... No, I'm not being stupid ... Don't you start getting your oar in ... Well, don't 'only' say ... What's it got to do with you? You come round here every Christmas, we don't see you the rest of the time ... What would *you* know about how we live? (*Husband scuttles out of kitchen, closely followed by your father*) Oh, that's right – walk away. That'll solve things ... (*Both head for the drink. Much shouting, bawling and high emotion emanates from kitchen*)

You, bursting into living room like a bullet out of gun, brushing down pinny, walking towards Grandma, who is still swaying along to Val.

You (*tersely*): We're having lunch at three now. (*Snatching away her sherry*) You can't watch the Queen's speech. We'll have to tape it.

TL (*emerging from shadowy corner*): Lunch is going to be that late? Oh, well, we can't stay now. We'll leave it this year. (*To your brother*) Come on. This isn't *my* idea of fun. (*Gathering up belongings, heads to door, back to you, dismissive wave over shoulder*) If we don't see you ... Happy New Year.

The contagion is unstoppable. There is no antidote. All hell breaks loose at Rosedean. Mum's got floury hands – from crushing her tranquillisers with the rolling pin. Dad's uncorking the wine – at seven in the morning. And you, siblings and spouses are pressed against the mullioned windows – of your secure psychiatric unit.

What she says

'We're not coming.'
'We're not going.'
'We're not staying.'

What you need to do

Get hold of her nail clippings and send them off to the School of Tropical Medicine. Hope they find the cure.

Bundle everyone into a Morris Minor, Von Trapp family-style, and head for the hills.

Introduce her to your distant cousins – the Borgias.

The Equaliser

What she does

Punishes you every day of your wretched life for having the barefaced temerity to *walk out on her* after you caught *her* dogging with *her* boss in the Morrisons car park.

What's more, this is a woman who a) never, in 11 years of marriage, had a kind word to say about you (does 'unbelievable' count?), b) never discovered the kitchen and would wait – until midnight, if necessary – for you to come home and feed her, c) never booked the same two weeks off in the summer as you and the children, and d) NEVER gave out.

Although, on the plus side, what she did do was: demean you in front of your friends (she was very good at that), taught the children to treat you with as much contempt as she did and spent many an hour expertly jabbing her finger in your face.

The question arises, not why did you leave but why did you stay? Who alone knows? The point is, you're out of it now. Or so you thought. She's got a different take on things: 'I didn't say you could go.' So now you're a marked man and she's on a full-time mission to Get Even.

First off, she employs the legal world's equivalent of autopsy showman Gunther von Hagens to bleed you dry.

Then she waltzes off with the house and all its contents – but not before you've handed over an extra 85 grand, because she wants to convert the garage into a panic room.

Finally! Her trump card. Mum's gone to Iceland. Her and the kids' new address is 24 Eyrarbakki Crescent, Siglufjordur. Makes access problematic? Exactly.

Heathrow, 3 a.m. Arrivals. You, clutching two helium balloons and a pair of gargantuan teddy bears, hopping up and down with barely suppressed exaltation. TE sweeps into the terminal. Sans enfants.

You (*looking past her at knee-height*): Where are the ... ?
TE: They're not coming.

You, mouth agape.

TE: Now, where will I get a decent coffee?
You (*recovering wits, slowly*): Where are the ... ?
TE: Have you got any sterling?
You (*coming to*): Am I ... ? What is ... ? So where are the kids? *Where are they?*
TE: They changed their minds.
You: Changed their minds!! Since the weekend? They were really excited about coming and seeing Nana and Grandad. (*Dawning realisation*) Everyone's coming to the house tomorrow. I've booked a magician. (*Small puff of steam*)

There's a cake with their faces on. (*Pressure rising*) There's 60 people arriving at my house at 4 o'clock this afternoon, expecting to see two kids celebrating their sixth birthday. (*Thar she blows!*) I PAID FOR THREE SEATS, NOT ONE, FROM REKYJAVIK TO HEATHROW. I HAVEN'T SEEN THEM FOR THREE MONTHS SINCE I TREKKED ALL THE WAY OVER THERE TO BE WITH THEM FOR THE ONE DAY YOU ALLOWED ME. YOU ARE NOT DOING THIS TO ME!

TE (*shrugging*): Who left whom?

Say the day finally arrives when you can think about having another woman in your life and you're not gasping for air from a brown paper bag. Don't relax. She's got other plans for your happy ever after ...

TE, sitting in Icelandic sitting room, rifling through a dossier, while issuing orders to you on the phone.

TE: ... so they both want the new Nintendos ... Get them couriered – I've said they're getting them tomorrow. Oh, and transfer that money to my new high interest account by the weekend ... So. How's it going with that woman you're seeing?

You: Oh ... erm. Yeah, fine. Listen, I'll let you go. I'll sort the Nintendos.

TE (*picking up piece of A4, studying it*): You seeing her this weekend?

You: No. Er ... No. I was supposed to be seeing her, but she can't make it.

TE (*flicking through file*): Is she the one renovating the house in Marazion?

You (*how does she know about that?*): Nnno ...

TE (*perusing file again*): Ahh. I'm thinking of the one with the dogs.

You: Did I tell you about her? She's just a friend ... married to a guy I work with.

TE (*tearing up piece of A4 along with photograph clipped to it. Clicks a slide projector, looks up at image of you and female frolicking in woodland*): Do you still manage to get up to Bluebell Woods?

You: Yeah, now and again. Why?

TE: Someone I know thought they saw you up there. You were with a girl. Hair tied up, green coat, dark handbag?

You: Who saw me?

TE: Can't remember. So is that the one you're seeing now?

You: No.

TE: Why not?

You: She's not here any more. She's gone with her job to ...

TE (*decisively, pushing round globe with her finger*): Cracow.

You: Hmmmm ... Anyway. What about you? Busy?

TE: Yes. Very busy. (*Picks up marker pen and strikes through typewritten screed*)

Busy? You bet. Tracking down any female who shows even a mote of interest in you and bad-mouthing every part of your being right down to the last molecule.

Even if you didn't have the children yoking you together, she'd still be sticking as close to you as a burr to a woollen walking sock. Remember? She Did Not Give You Permission to Leave.

What she says

'You didn't have to go.'
'I wasn't the one who broke up the family.'
'I didn't hold a gun to your head.' (She did, actually.)

What you need to do

Make like Catherine Zeta-Jones in *Entrapment*. From now on it's a black Lycra bodysuit and balaclava and limbo moves to avoid her laser sights.

Marry her sister. (In female society, it's the equivalent of setting off a small thermo-nuclear device under the rim of her toilet seat. This only works if she's got a sister.)

On the rare occasions you have the kids on holiday, take them to a Parental Deprogramming Centre to be fed subliminal messages saying, 'Mummy's a whore and a bitch.'

Chapter Five

Friends

Miss-Fortune Teller

What she does

Delights in your disasters. No, really she does. Yes, she's presented herself to you as your friend. She actually looks and sounds like one as well. But let's look closer at the evidence.

Exhibit A. Your husband's frozen the joint account and legged it with a hairdresser-turned-life coach, your guaranteed-to-make-you-a-million business proposal is lying in shreds in the skip, and you are seconds from phoning Brangelina to see if they'll add your children to their 'rainbow'.

Luckily, you can rely on your friends to help you through your life crisis. Except this one. Sure, she'll be the first one on the phone when news leaks out and, because you're vulnerable and trusting, you'll spill the beans. You'll confide, you'll cry, you'll complain, you'll cry, you'll catastrophise, you'll cry.

Stop it. Right now. Because Miss-Fortune Teller is on the other end of the line, biting her knuckles with glee, barely able to contain her excitement at the good news that you're having such a bad time.

MFT, on phone, arms clasped around hunched-up knees, in manner of coiled spring, about to explode with joy. Looks skywards and mouths, 'Thank you, God' as she revels in your rollcall of wretchedness.

You: ... it's an absolute nightmare. I cannot believe he could do this to me. I don't know whether I should keep it all from the kids or what ... I just don't understand what he's playing at ... and then, to top it all, to get *that* happen as well ...

MFT: Mmmm ... you poor thing. (*Give me more detail, you bitch*)

You: ... oh, and, of course, she's 25, isn't she? A 25-year-old life coach, well she's screwed up mine good and proper. Thank you very much ...

MFT: Is she attractive? (*I hope so*)

You: Er ... erm ... well, probably. But, anyway, I just don't know what to do for money, the boys are going to need more football kit soon, there's a school trip I've promised they can go on. Is he going to cough up for all that? I don't think so. No, it'll be me, even though he's the one who ...

MFT: So are you really going to be struggling financially? (*I hope so*)

You: Oh, I don't know. It's just going to be so tough ... Do you know what, I just feel ...

MFT: Suicidal?

You: No, not that bad, but do I need any more examples that

Miss-Fortune Teller

life is tough? I get the bloody hint. It's tough. Just wish one good thing would happen, just one ...
MFT: Mmmm ... poor you. (*Right, got everything I need now, so get off the phone, I've got people to call*)

You're standing on the abyss; *she's* pulled up a deckchair to sit and wait for you to topple over. No matter how disappointing her life is, at least it's nowhere near as bad as yours. Yippee! The universe is on her side, after all! *Schadenfreude* doesn't even come close.

Heaven help you, though, if you manage to crawl back from the edge. You've got a new man, moved up a postcode, Brangelina can whistle for your lovely boys, and people are falling over themselves to invest in your Big Idea. What's more, the life coach has drawn up her own 'Values, Beliefs and Core Aims' checklist – and it doesn't include your ex-husband.

MFT on phone, looking skywards, furious.

You: ...can't believe how it's all turned around, the boys are settled, *he's* gorgeous, that's all going very well, and we all feel really at home here. The garden's huge – did I tell you we've got a little nest of baby blackbirds ...
MFT: ... Mmmmm, lovely. So, is your ex helping with the mortgage?

You: Er ... no, we're renting.

MFT (*phew*): Oh, that's okay then, so long as the landlord doesn't want to sell in the near future, I suppose.

You: Well, they haven't really said. But the main thing is it's great for the schools and we're close to town. No more school run!

MFT: God, how early do you have to get them all up to walk there?! You're up near that retail park that's closing down, aren't you?

You: No, oh, I know what you're thinking, no, we didn't go for that house, we're much nearer the station end, backing onto the green ...

MFT (*not happy*): Oh, right. Bit noisy with the trains.

You: Yeah, that's the one drawback.

MFT: Thought so. (*Got you*)

You: But, anyway, it is lovely because we don't feel like we're in the thick of things ...

MFT: Well, where we are, of course, we really *do* have the best of all possible worlds, it's rural *and* it's a ten-minute commute to the city. I can be in the West End in no time, but always, always glad to get back to my own little home. Can't beat your own bricks and mortar. How are you all finding it being there together? Is he alright with the boys? Must be difficult, someone new coming into a family – I always wonder how men cope with that sort of thing ... Anyway, great to talk to you, got to dash and get myself tarted up, we're off up to town to the opera tonight. (*Beat that. You cow*)

Suddenly, your sought-after postcode feels like the fag end of the Monopoly board, you're looking at your big-hearted, lovely, liberated new man and wondering if you've let a child-beater across your threshold, and you realise your only chance of a big night out is taking the bread down the garden to the birds.

What she says

'I'm always here for you.' (*Only if it's bad news, though.*)
'Poor you/poor thing/what a pity/what a shame/isn't that awful.' (*Ha ha ha ha ha.*)
'That's great. So, it's all worked out then.' (*Bollocks.*)

What you need to do

Get yourself a PR who can spin faster than Alistair Campbell.
Wear a burkha to the housing benefits office.
Have the best life ever – that'll finish her off.

Commander-in-Chief

What she does

Treats her chums like cannon fodder. You think she's your best friend. And then she's not. And then she is again. And then she's someone else's. Whatever you do, you can't win, because she's got a secret underground bunker where she plots her manoeuvres. That's 'relationships' to you and me.

Normal idea of friendship: you meet someone; you like them; find you've got something in common – they iron their knickers, you iron your knickers. Bingo! Friends for life.

CiC's idea of friendship: she's the puppet master; you're the puppet. She's the ventriloquist, you're the dummy. But you'll have absolutely no idea she's working you from behind.

This is how it will start. You've already got friends – good and loyal ones. But she'll outfriend them. Quickly, quietly and efficiently – by appointing herself your Chief Buddy.

Suddenly, a woman whose existence you weren't even aware of last week is Always There for You. She's the one constantly available for a late-night pep talk. Here she is, popping up at your hospital bedside when you've had your gallstones removed. Here she is again, clasping your elbow at your dad's funeral. Before you know it, you're as dependent on her as a tramp on White Lightning.

Just as well, because she's stealthily dispatched all your other friends like a commando on night patrol. But this isn't so bad – after all, she's *such* a great ally. Hold on! Who's that she's having coffee with at *your* favourite cafe? Isn't that your former best friend – the one CiC steered you away from because she was 'two-faced'? And what's this all about?! Why haven't *you* been invited to her mulled wine melee? And ... you what! She's taking someone *else* to Michael Bublé!

You're going to have to ask her what's going on. You may even whimper, 'Don't you like me any more?' Oh, thank the Lord above and all the saints, a beneficent smile lights up her kindly face as she says, 'Is that what you thought? Don't be daft. I don't have as much in common with anyone else as I do with you. We're like sisters.' Phew, you're still her number one friend.

Hang on. Now she's blanking you. Is she? Yes, yes she is. She can't be. She bloody well is. Ah, no, no, here she is on your doorstep with a bottle of wine and an empathetic air.

Woah! Wait a minute, she's off again. Where's she gone

now? You were supposed to be having Darjeeling and Jamaica Inn ginger cake (with custard). Pah! More chance of getting an audience with the Pope. Oh, it's okay, it's okay, it's okay. She's back again. Oh, she's gone. No wait, back. No, gone. In, out, in, out, off, on, up, down. It's the Hokey *fricking* Cokey. You may as well be Christopher Walken, wearing a sweaty bandana, because she's unmasked herself as the Vietcong, gleefully forcing you and your compatriots to play Russian Roulette – purely for her own entertainment.

Friday. The high street. You, trudging home from work, with free newspaper and a carton of milk, passing by the steamy windows of the Nek n Thai. Momentarily glancing at your dismal reflection, you spot, through the one clear patch of glass, CiC, surrounded by your friends at a banquet-laden table, heads thrown back in merry abandon. CiC clocks you. You scurry.

CiC (*coolly calling after you from the doorway*): Hi!
You: H-Hi! Erm, just on my way to erm ... but, anyway, how are you? Just got to erm, got to erm ... erm ...
CiC: Where have you got to go?
You: I'm ... errr ... I'm in such a rush, I've got to drop these (*holding out milk and paper*) ... and then errrm ...
CiC: What?

You: Got to go back to the errr ... got to go back to the errrm ...and just finish something at the office.
CiC: It's eight o'clock.
You: I know ... err ... slave drivers! So, anyway, I'll err, how are you?
CiC: Yeah, fine.
You: So. (*Pointing lamely at the Nek n Thai group*) Anyway, won't keep you ...
CiC: Oh, okay. (*Suddenly reaching out, laying a cold hand upon yours*) Are you alright?
You (*obliterated, blitzed, annihilated*): Fine.
CiC: Good. Bye then.

What she says

'You're my best friend.' (You're not.)
'She did say she found you a bit aloof.' (She didn't.)
'I'll never tell anyone that.' (She already has.)

What you need to do

Next time she's bitching about X, ask her to clarify if that's the same X she had a 'deep spiritual connection' with last Thursday.

Hold a kangaroo court and charge her with: grievous verbal harm, using a weapon (sarcasm) and taking without consent (your friends).

Join the real army. They'll teach you how to garrotte silently.

The Spadist

What she does

Has no use for tact or diplomacy – leaves all that to the likes of Kofi Annan. She prefers the sledgehammer approach. Got a nasty cough? 'I knew someone who died of that.' Your husband's just walked out? 'Well, you have let yourself go.' Suffering from a bout of clinical depression? 'You do bring it on yourself.' Family just been wiped out? 'You'll get over it.'

Why on earth isn't she observing the rules of social engagement? No fun, is it? This way she gets to, by turns, crush or inflame you. Her cutting barbs will either have you crawling quietly away to a corner, or taking the bait, leaving you to face the charges of wounding with intent. Either way, she wins.

The s(p)adist will tell you that you have to be cruel to be kind, when in fact she's just being cruel. She maintains she's speaking for everyone when she tells you that, yes, you probably are unemployable, or no, you're not imagining it; there are massive bags under your eyes, and yes, it is your child the others don't want to play with.

She doesn't just call a spade a spade, she calls it a JCB digger. What she doesn't realise is that while she's extolling the virtues of Spadism, most people around are thinking, 'What I'd give for a spade right now. I'd cleave her bloody bonce in.'

She prides herself on being straight talking, no nonsense, telling it like it is, tough, uncompromising, honest and genuine. Reality? She's just a bitch.

Her stings and sneers are always dressed up as integrity and courage. Only she has the guts to say out loud 'what everyone else is thinking'. How brave, how noble. Except the reason no one else says it is because it's hurtful, mean and insensitive – and usually makes people cry.

You, coming out of chemist. TS coming at you out of nowhere.

TS: Hi there. Just bumped into your sister.
You: Oh, right.
TS: She's lost loads of weight.
You: I know. She's looking great.
TS: *I* don't think so. I think she's looking gaunt.
You: No, I think she looks fantastic.
TS: Doesn't suit her. She's too tall.
You: Everyone thinks she looks great.
TS: She looks like a bloody great beanpole!
You: No, she doesn't!
TS: Oh come on, what with her mad hair, she looks like Worzel Gummidge now!

The Spadist

You, speechless.

TS: What has she done to herself? Why would you want to lose weight to end up looking like Russell Brand if you're a girl?

You (*crossly*): Everyone thinks she looks really pretty. I'd love to be her height. She's got a supermodel figure, she can get away with wearing anything she likes. Who wouldn't want to look like her.

TS: Hmmmm ... those bloody great feet of hers.

Take note, though: the Spadist will not appreciate you responding with even a milligram of directness towards her.

You, unloading washing machine, loading tumble dryer, unloading dishwasher, loading TS with tea and biscuits.

TS: I didn't get that job I went for.
You: What job?
TS: Keep up. The one I told you about.
You (*separating whites*): Which one? I didn't know you were going for a job.
TS: Oh, yes, forgot – you have babies. You can't remember anything.
You (*little laugh*): Okay, but I'm sure you didn't tell me.
TS: I did.
You: Sorry, sorry, what was the job again?
TS: Head buyer.

You: Which department?
TS: Wine.
You: Oh ... I see.
TS: What, what do you see?
You: I know you really love your wine, you know an awful lot more about it than I do. But it's quite a highly qualified job, isn't it? People think it isn't, but it is.
TS: What? So I'm not highly qualified?
You: Oh, no, you really know your stuff. But perhaps they needed someone who'd done something similar before.
TS: I'm secretary of the local wine circle.
You: Oh, yes, I know, that's brilliant. I'm sure you could do it.
TS: I could have done it with my eyes closed. Their loss.
You: You're right and even if they weren't looking for someone with formal qualifications, you can sometimes go into those interviews and your face just doesn't fit. It happens to all of us.
TS: Ooooh miaaaaowwww! Remind me not to come to you again if I need a bit of constructive criticism.

What she says

'I'm not a people pleaser.' (We know.)

'You either love me or you loathe me.' (Guess what ...!)

'I'm not scared of offending people.' (Like that's a good thing?)

What you need to do

Send her to the Middle East – her 'telling it like it is' will go down a storm there.

Stop slathering on the body lotion. You'll need skin as tough as an alligator.

Measure her up for a scold's bridle.

Mag Hag

What she does

Lives her life according to the Ten Commandments handed down by the editors of glossy magazines. Her world is one long round of spas, shoes, lip gloss, pedicures, colonic irrigation, yoga, pilates, botox, detox, big bags, little bags, skinny jeans, flared jeans, straight hair, curly hair, smock tops, tight tops, Peacocks and Hobbs. And that's just Monday.

She hasn't got a life, she's got a lifestyle. She thinks she's Carrie Bradshaw from *Sex and the City*, and she's so shallow she might evaporate. She doesn't 'do' loyalty, she's not 'into' emotional support. Her idea of friends is *Friends*. If she says, 'I'll be there for you', don't take it as a heartfelt gesture, it's just something she heard Rachel say to Monica. You will only remain her friend so long as your bag complements her shoes.

Her holidays, restaurants, films, books, homes, furnishings, cars and food will revolve around what her magazine of choice dictates is in or out. So one moment she will go on an ironic weekend to Southend-on-Sea; the next a Tibetan retreat with a quick stopover to see the Dalai Lama because he (or is it a she? MH isn't quite sure) is apparently big on enlightenment. Or something.

She'll attempt to read the serious pages in her mag — female circumcision, the growing sex slave industry, that sort of thing, but only on public transport. The minute she's left alone with her beloved bible, however, it's straight to the Summer Shoe Special.

To compensate for a lack of identity, she smothers herself in labels.

MH, catwalking her way into café.

You: Oh, you look nice.
MH: Thanks, yeah, it's just a few new pieces.
You: I thought I hadn't seen that top before, it's lovely.
MH: It's off the shoulder but accentuates my neckline. What I've done is to focus the attention down towards the waistline by nipping it in with a bang-on-trend wider belt because I am the classic pear shape. Think Beyoncé ... think J-Lo.
You: Oh.
MH: So the definition of the skirt is then balanced, which then draws the eye down towards my best feature, which is my calves, and the higher shoes enhance that. And then the little bag is, I guess, a little twist, a little surprise that maybe you wouldn't expect.

Mag Hag

You (*God, there's a famine in Darfur*): So, where did you get the top?

MH: The top is a Marc Demarchelier, the fedora is a Gobblerancia, the cape a Morecambe and Vyse, the skirt, Dada, the cane, Sushiama Sushiota, belt by the Mitford sisters, tights, Mavis Pablo, shoes, well, Jimmy Riddle, natch.

If you have the misfortune to live in the real world, where people get ill, lose their jobs, put on weight or suffer from depression, her only concern is, 'Has this been covered in a magazine?' Breast cancer? Tick. (*There's a lovely designer T-shirt to show you care.*) Homelessness? Tick. (*Princess Diana did that. Make sure they don't get too close, though.*) Global Warming? Tick. (*Great concerts and a fab opportunity to show off your pink designer wellies.*)

On the other hand ... Bowel cancer? I don't think so. (*There's nothing sexy about colons.*) The elderly? Hmmm ... maybe. (*Vintage is in.*) Economic migration? (*What the heck does that mean?*)

A trendy bar. MH, sipping on a JD and Goji berry juice. You, knocking back 500ml beaker of wine.

MH: What's wrong with you?
You: Really bad news.
MH: Damn, is the Issey Miyake sale over?

You: I've got cancer.

MH (*phew*): Oh dear.

You: It's okay, though. They've caught it very early on – it's an excellent prognosis.

MH: Good, good (*I'm bored now*). Will you have to have chemotherapy?

You: Not sure. Probably.

MH: Will you lose your hair?

You: I don't know.

MH: Let's hope not (*because you're not coming out with me if you do*). Look on the bright side though ...

You: Yes, I'm trying to stay positive ...

MH: ...you might lose loads of weight!

What she says

'It's bang on trend.' (This could be anything from a sandwich to a car.)

'Gordon Brown? Is he the new black?'

'I'm loving it/It's so now, so then, last season, five minutes ago/Purleeeeze/I've so gotta have it/OmiGod!/To die for/Bad hair day/Empowering/Killer heels/Shoes, shoes, shoes, shoes, shoes, shoes, shoes, shoes.'

What you need to do

Get your 'key pieces' from the back of those supplements that fall out of the Sunday papers, i.e., the uni-slipper, patterned tabard and taupe slacks. See her clattering off in her Louboutin shoes.

Give her some fake perfume you got off the market, which smells like wee and brings her out in a rash.

Tell her you've got her a 'timeless', 'vintage', 'retro' bag. It's a tartan shopping trolley.

The Foul Weather Friend

What she does

Walks with you in the vale of tears. She's the one there for you in the bad times, when you're lonely, scared, depressed, poor, helpless, hopeless and hapless. She understands life's a struggle. How fantastic to have such an empathetic mate.

But the empathy lasts only as long as you're sliding along skid row together. Sure, it's nice to have someone in the gutter with you, but she's got her foot on your neck so you can't look up at the stars.

She has a vested interest in keeping you miserable, because her own life is as bleak as a hobo convention in Vange. Yours wasn't as bad as that – you could raise the odd chuckle of an evening. But she's not having that: you're now an honorary member of her doom and gloom club.

The mistake you made was in assuming she had your best interests at heart. You were the bird with the broken wing. But she's not taking you to the PDSA – she's keeping you in a box and watching while you suffocate.

The Duck and Dosser. You, walking back from bar with two halves of lager and black towards FWF, slumped in sagging sofa.

You: By the way, good news at last.

FWF (*oh, God*): What?
You: I've come up on the lottery.
FWF (*nervously*): You're joking, right?
You: It's not much ...
FWF (*phew*): How much?
You: £500. Hey, maybe my luck's changing. It could be me!
FWF (*I don't think so*): What are you going to do with it?
You: Ohhh, massage, spa, Bond Street, holiday ... world's my oyster.
FWF: Really?! Nothing for the needy then?
You: Well. *I'm* a bit needy.
FWF: No, seriously, though. You remember we once said if you ever got rich ...
You: I'm hardly rich.
FWF: Richer than me. You did say you'd always sponsor a child in Bangladesh. That's not just a child, that's a school, a village and a goat.
You: Well, I could give away some of it, I suppose.
FWF: How much?
You: A bit.
FWF: Just a bit?
You: I don't know. Half? Two thirds? How much do you think they need?
FWF: All of it, of course.
You (*crestfallen, sighing*): But I deserve a little bit of it ...

FWF: Typical! Everyone's the same. Come into a bit of money, principles go out the window.
You: Oh dear, it is a bit selfish. I'd only spend it on more clothes.
FWF: Quite. And it's all the little Bangladeshis who are going blind making them anyway. Ha ha. I'm really proud of you. We paupers have to stick together.

That's you back in the workhouse with your friend. No parole. Both single, skint and suffering in sisterhood. But wait! What's this? Providence delivers unto you a potential suitor.

Lidl's café. Saturday morning. You, carrying two filter coffees back to FWF.

You: Good news!
FWF (*not again*): What?
You: I'm going on a date ...
FWF: Uh-huh?
You: With a man!
FWF: What man?
You: My brother-in-law's friend, divorced, no children, all his own hair and teeth. Getting a good feeling about this one.
FWF: How long has he been divorced?
You: About a year.

FWF (*sucking in air*): Baggage.
You: At our age everyone's got baggage.
FWF: Why no children?
You: Don't know. Perhaps *she* didn't want any.
FWF: Or *he* didn't.
You (*faltering*): I don't know.
FWF: You remember you once said ...
You: I haven't even been out with him yet.
FWF: You once said you wouldn't even go on a date with a man who didn't want children.
You: Yeah but ...
FWF: He hasn't got children.
You: He might want them now.
FWF: He might not.
You: I don't know what to do now. I can't very well ask my brother-in-law if this guy wants kids.
FWF: No, you can't.
You: I'm going to have to ...
FWF: Leave it?
You (*despondent*): Yeah, leave it.
FWF: Well done! We're not going to settle for second best.

See? She knows you better than you know yourself. You thought you were just a bit 'fed up'. She reminds you that you have always had a genetic predisposition for misery.

You admit you can be slightly 'negative' at times, she'll diagnose it as a depressive episode; you confess you sometimes 'fail to see the bright side', she tells you you're bipolar.

Still at least you're in this together. Well, you are until Dame Fortune smiles on *her*, then she's out of there faster than Usain Bolt off the blocks ... 'Hang on!' you cry after her ever diminishing figure as it disappears over the horizon. 'Isn't it supposed to be us against the world?'

'You're joking, misery guts. I'm out of here.'

What she says

'Life's a bitch. And then you die ...'

' ... yeah, there's an afterlife ... ten times worse than this ...'

' ... and what's more, it's for all eternity.'

What you need to do

Sit her down. Tell her to prepare herself for the worst. Then burst out laughing.

Always look on the bright side.

Leave her in the gutter.

Chapter Six
Neighbours and Local Folk

Lord of the Manor

What he does

Lords it over all and sundry. You'd better call Time Team – you've been whisked back to the Middle Ages. It doesn't matter that Elizabeth II is on the throne, feudal laws still apply in his fiefdom.

You thought you'd moved into a modern-day commuter village with high-speed links to King's Cross and easy access to the M25. Where did it say in the house deeds that you'd signed over your liberty, your land rights, your access, your maidenhead and your right to keep your own chutney?

He's the pub brute, holding court, fat, unlit cigar in hand, signalling to other customers when they may enter his presence.

You, at bar, holding your £20 note aloft. LotM in far corner, blocking fireplace, surrounded by press-ganged entourage.

You: Bacardi and Coke, please.

LotM (*booming*): Oooh ... Bacardi and Coke, eh? Very sophisticated.

You nod and smile.

LotM: The new girl in town likes a Bacardi. Better keep an eye on her. (*Guffaws and giggles from coterie*)

You smile and nod.

LotM: Oi! Get yourself over here.
You: Actually, I'm just waiting for my ...
LotM: Well, you can come and wait over here.
You: No, really, I'm fine here, thanks.
LotM: It's not an option, love. (*Swaggers over to bar, hitching waistband up, picks up your Bacardi, plonks it on his table. Turns back to bar and whistles*) Bring your nuts.

He owns you now, along with everybody else in Lower Upitself. Naturally, his background in a Stevenage semi was the perfect preparation for his role as Lord of the Manor. He strides about the village like a latter-day squire, in Hunter wellies and a Barbour, trailing two gundogs at his heels. If he passes you in the street, don't forget to doff your cap.

He's invented his own hierarchy. He's at the top. You, along with everybody else, are at the bottom. You will be in no doubt of this because he doesn't do servile, i.e., holding open doors, standing in queues, or even talking at a reasonable volume. He bellows. But then you would, if you wanted to make your voice heard from the scullery to the bell tower.

You might have some high-falutin' media job 'up in London'. But your status on his 'estate' is lower than a swineherd's. You might have a few friends around for brandy and mince pies, with him it's nothing less than 20,000 square feet of marquee. There's a three-line whip to his festive feast, complete with wassailing minstrels, flagons of Bordeaux, a boar on a spit – and the invitation says Fancy Dress. Tough, you're wearing a wimple.

It's his turf, his rules. Having a nice little Sunday pootle round the lanes? Watch out! Get your Daewoo in the hedgerow. He's coming through in a Land Rover the size of a space shuttle. Thought you had a secluded garden? There's his fat, oafish, flat-capped fizzog bobbing over your mimosa. Planning a weekend away? Not without *his* approval.

You and partner, at food-ordering till, LotM on stool, having requisitioned entire drinking section of bar.

You: A pint of Groused Rat. And a Bacardi and Coke, please.
LotM (*booming*): There they are. Where've you two been hiding? Been keeping a low profile, haven't you?
You: Just been a bit busy at work ... and getting organised for a holiday.
LotM (*bigger booming*): So what are you providing for the Summer Beanfeast? Seen the posters haven't you? Put a flier through your door last week.

You: Well ... we're not going to be here. We're off to the Languedoc for a couple of weeks.

LotM: Langue what? Listen, we need cakes. You girls are good at baking. Get yourself in the kitchen before you go.

You: I honestly won't have the time ...

LotM (*to coterie*): What else do we need? Oh yeah, you've got an allotment. We always have a big fruit and veg stall. You know – huge parsnips, enormous marrows, big pumpkins (*leering at you*). Know what I mean?

You (*under breath to partner*): Right, finish your drink. Come on. We're going. I've had enough of him. (*Turning to crowd*) Listen, we're off. Bye, everyone. See you soon.

LotM (*swaggers towards to you, hands outstretched. Suddenly – and without warning – cups both hands under your bust and jiggles your breasts about*): And we could do with some lovely melons like these.

Oh, so he's not so ignorant about France after all - well, he certainly seems to know what droit de seigneur means. Face it, you'll always be the vassal and his wife. You may have a cutting-edge, minimalist home. But it's still a peasant's cottage. Don't forget to curtsey.

Lord of the Manor

What he says

'Get off my land.'
'Dismissed.'
'How much for that royal crest?'

What you need to do

Organise a Peasants' Revolt.
Bring back the guillotine.
Declare your house a Free Republic.

The Inconvenient Storekeeper

What he does

Runs a convenience store. Surely, by definition, that means a store at your convenience, 24/7. 'Hello, my good man. Do you have any radishes I can purchase?' 'I certainly do. They're right here. Day or night, you are welcome into my store to peruse my shelves. From pot noodle to tin foil, I've got the lot. That's what I'm here for. That's why I run a convenience store.'

You would think.

So why is it when you ask him where he keeps his custard creams, it's as if you've pointed a Kalashnikov at his forehead, told him you've got his children locked up in the boot of your car and are about to dump them in the nearest quarry?

Does he run a shop or an examination board? Everything is met with a disapproving sigh. 'Where do you keep the sugar?' Wrong question. 'Do you have any brown sauce?' Failed. 'Do you sell peanuts?' Do not pass the tills. You have been known to half starve rather than run the gauntlet of the IS.

'Haven't you got anything smaller?' is his stock phrase. Even if you handed over an old halfpenny, it wouldn't be small enough.

And don't hold your hand out for the change. There's about as much chance of him touching you as he would a leper. Your pennies will be hurled down on the counter. Preferably – for him – one might bounce off the corner and catch you in the eye.

Ask him if he's got anything you could carry your 90 items home in and he will present one wafer-thin bag designed to disintegrate the minute you put anything in it heavier than a feather duster. Deep sighing will ensue as he watches you attempt to retrieve your groceries from every corner of his shop. As you roll around like a deranged octopus, he merely instructs other customers to step over you.

Why is he a storekeeper? He hates, in no particular order: tins of food, newspapers, booze, milk, cleaning products, frozen goods, toiletries, customers, cash, tills, aisles, cheques, baskets, and the little sign that says 'Open'.

It should be simple; he sells things, you buy them. But no. You are now in an abusive relationship. You're doing relaxation tapes over breakfast to steel yourself to buy a copy of the *Daily Mirror*. You've learned to adapt to the taste of hot water rather than purchase teabags and milk. You look up corner shops in the local directory in the hope that he isn't the only one in a ten-mile radius. Eventually, you will need a cognitive behavioural therapist to go with you just to buy a bar of soap.

His poxy little 'empire' is one step up from a garage kiosk. You do wonder how he makes a living when he seems to be allergic to customers and money.

The store. IS, leaning forward, knuckles on counter, watching, as you approach.

You (*tiny voiced*): Just the chewing gum, please.
IS: Is that it?
You (*twitchy*): Yes, thank you.
IS: It's not even worth me opening the till.
You: Oh, I've got the right money.
IS (*sucks his teeth*): Don't you need anything else?
You (*starting to sweat*): Erm ... I ... don't ... think ... I ...
IS (*aggressively*): What, you don't need any milk? Got all the butter you need? Fridge full of food?
You (*do I need milk? Do I? Do I? I do. I do. I do*): Erm ... Ah ... Have you got semi-skimmed?

IS nods head at fridge.

You (*returning to counter with milk and bread as back-up*): That's it then, thanks. (*He's going to let me go now*)

IS sucks teeth again.

You: Oh, God, of course, I need ham, don't I? (*Is that right? Do I need ham?*)
IS: Four pound 15.
You: Lovely. Going to have to pay on this now. (*Handing over debit card*)
IS: Five quid.
You: Oh ... er, what?
IS (*heavy sighing*): Has to be more than five quid on a card.
You: (*I'm never going to get out. I'm never going to get out of this shop. Ever.*) You keep the card.

Or:

You: Good morning. Just wondered if I could get a packet of those up there?
IS: Up there?
You: Yes, please.
IS: Those up there?
You (*twitchy*): Erm ... is that ... okay?

IS sucks teeth.

You: Do you have any lower down?

IS: No.
You: I think I probably will need those up there then, please.

IS sucks teeth.

You (*nervously*): Have you got something ...? Perhaps ... you could ... erm ... something to, perhaps? ... erm get them down with?

IS shakes head.

You: Actually, don't worry. Thanks for your help ... I probably don't need toilet rolls today ... (*They managed with newspaper squares in the old days ...*)

What he says

'If you can't see them, I haven't got them.'
'Leave that outside.' (*That's* your baby.)
'You again.'

What you need to do

Wear a big coat and steal stuff.

Write a letter to the local paper, extolling his virtues as the friendliest shopkeeper in town, drawing attention to the fact he will go out of his way to help and only stocks fresh organic produce, and that no delivery is too small or too far.

Take your time – spend hours and hours up and down the aisles, take a sandwich and a flask of tea, enquire frequently of his stock, read all the magazines cover to cover. Then leave, without purchasing a single thing.

The Border Guard

What she does

Thinks your flat is an extension of hers. You're moving in: boxes are piled high everywhere; six removal men are swigging tea; the kids are going doolally over who's having which bedroom; a sweaty BT engineer perches on a box marked 'fragile', stuck into *The Star*; you're on the patio, wondering how it's gone from looking like a lush Hawaiian oasis to a barren rain-soaked wasteland.

'Coooo-eeee!' A woman you've never laid eyes on before stands on your polar-white sheepskin rug in her wellies. Before you can get the 'Wh ...' out in 'Who ...?' a monologue begins:

BG: Now then. I live upstairs from you. Got to know your builder quite well. So let's see what he's done. (*She breezes past you, on her way to the kitchen. You remain in living room, listening to sounds of cupboard doors opening and closing*) Mmmm, not as big as I thought. Ooh, where's the fridge? (*Doors now being slammed*) Oh, he's put it there. (*You remain in living room, briefly catching a glimpse of her as she heads to the bathroom*) Where's the light? (*Sounds of toilet being flushed and taps turned off and on*) Oh, I see, hot and cold from the one tap, mmm don't know if I'd have ... (*You remain in living room, briefly catching a glimpse of her again as she makes for the master bedroom*) Lilac? Hmmm. Oh you're getting that mould coming through under the window ... (*Rejoins you, where you remain standing in living room*) I'm sure you'll get it sorted. Now, I can't stop today, but I'll be able to pop over again tomorrow afternoon for a cup of tea. (*BG exits to hall, pauses on threshold and whistles*) Here, boy! (*A golden retriever, with filthy paws, trots out after her*)

Who the ...? What the ...? How the ...? Why the ...? Oh, you'll find out. You didn't realise neighbourhood watch meant she was watching the neighbours.

You, coming out of flat. BG, hovering in communal hall.

You: Oh, hello.
BG: Is that your Vauxhall Corsa, blue one, registration HG04 HXT?
You: Er, yes ...
BG: Only I saw someone else getting out of it on Tuesday, 11.10 a.m. That's when you're at work, isn't it?
You: Oh, I left it at my sister's the other night and she was just dropping it round.
BG: Blonde?
You: Erm, yes.

BG: Doesn't look at all like you.
You: It *was* my sister.
BG: Hmmm ... people park here that don't actually live here.
You: It *was* my sister.
BG: I've just noticed, your door. Not the same as everybody else's, is it? Anyway, I can't stop here all morning, got to go up to the second floor.
You (*barely audible*): It *was* my sister.

She's the self-appointed concierge/security guard/bouncer of your sweet homestead. Before long, you realise that 'communal' means 'mine' in her vocabulary.

The living room of your flat. You, alone, on the sofa, gesticulating angrily.

You (*ranting*): ...how *dare* you assume that you know what's best for me. I am sick and tired of your domineering, bossy behaviour ... (*faltering*). Actually. ACTUALLY, do you know what you are? A bully. You've been doing this since we were children. Well, *no more!* (*Theatrical wave of hand, standing up to face front window*) Oh ... oh, you may well look at me like that (*addressing the window*). No, no, it's time you heard me out. I've never had a voice in our family, thanks to you, well, listen to me *now* (*pointing proudly at self*). Yeah, ha, that's what I'm going to say to her, oh she's never seen that side of me, she thinks I'm a walkover, well, push me too far and you get *this* (*thumbs firmly jabbed at face*). Oh yes, she's had it coming for a long time, and you know it (*looking up, pointing at God*). Oh yes, that's it, right I'm ringing her now … grrrrr … oh yes, oh yes, I'm going to do it now while I'm angry (*high-fiving air*). Right … phone … phone, call her now … (*Wheeling round, small jump*) Aaaaagh!

BG (*leaning, arms folded, against the lounge wall, just by the ajar patio door*): Neighbourhood Watch. Seven o'clock. Bring a chair. (*Exits through open patio door*)

You'll soon learn to sweep the perimeter of your flat to check for intruders before conducting any conversations you may wish to have – especially those with yourself.

Taking diabolical liberties is her bread and butter. You may want to rethink giving her the key to water your plants while you're away – she's likely to book her son, his wife and some friends of theirs into the best B and B in town, i.e., your flat. (It's a bit of a squeeze at hers.)

One day you'll wake up in bed and … 'Morning!'

What she says

'Cooooeee!'

'It's alright. I've let myself in.'

'Don't mind me. You just get yourself off to bed if you want.'

What you need to do

Check out your lease to see if it allows for the construction of moats.

You know she didn't approve of your front door because it was 'different'? Well, make it really different, courtesy of your local constabulary: three-foot-thick, reinforced steel and one of those little eye-level slidy things you've seen them whipping back and forth on *The Bill*.

Install a cattle grid outside her front door. She'll never get across it in her mules.

Mummy Dearest

What she does

Controls the playground. There's more bullying coming from her direction than you'll ever see among the mini-despots in plimsolls. Don't think now you're all grown up you're safe: one encounter with her and you'll be calling ChildLine quicker than a smelly kid who stammers.

Remember that dreaded Sunday night feeling? The nausea that accompanied the opening bars of the *Antiques Roadshow*? Well, here we go again. It's still the *Antiques Roadshow*, except this time you can't wangle a sick note off your mum – you *are* the mum. *Déjà* bloody *vu*, as you may recall your French teacher saying.

Monday morning, a bright cheery day, your little ones are skipping towards the school gates, you are sick with nerves. Your seven-year-old takes you gently by the hand and tells you, 'Don't worry, Mum. Be brave, you just have to stand up to her.'

Any shred of courage you'd mustered disintegrates as you move closer to St Aloysius's. The gatekeeper awaits. Is she going to say hello today? Ah, not today. In fact, she's looking at you as if you've been caught slipping crack cocaine through the fence to the nursery children.

Mummy Dearest

She was the class bitch when she was nine and has been hankering to retain the title ever since. The only reason she had kids was to get back in charge of the school gates.

Every day, there she is, in the midst of her St Aloysius 'Masseeve'; a submissive, terrified clique of thirtysomethings. But she hasn't forgotten *you*. You're booked in for a 3.15 p.m. mess-with-your-mind session.

3.15 p.m. At the school entrance. Your best friend – and ally – is off sick. You're on your own. MD approaches from behind. Your neck bristles.

You: (*Oh my God. Is that her? Is she coming near me? Is she going to talk to me? Oh my God. Oh my God.*)
MD: Hiya!
You (*gulp*): Oh, hi ...
MD: Had to laugh yesterday ...
You (*relaxing*): Oh yes?
MD: ...your youngest.
You (*laughing insouciantly*): What?
MD: He's a little character, isn't he?
You (*tensing fractionally*): Mmmmm ...
MD: Even when I saw him last Thursday in the vole tabard, he was still kicking off. Ha ha.
You: A vole what?
MD (*dismissively*): Oh, you know. It's for the disruptive ones.

They have to wear it when they're sent to the Contemplation Corner. The staff are very good, though, they're very patient, even when he lashes out.

You: Lashes out ...?

MD: Well, it's common sense. Otherwise he's going to really hurt someone one day. Luckily, the other children leave him alone. I don't think that's a problem, though. It's just as well he's a bit of a bookworm, otherwise he'd be upset about not being picked for the football. Tell you what, credit to him, he's got a tremendous appetite. Does he get that from you? (*Looking you up and down*)

You: We've never had a problem with him being fussy.

MD: He'll end up looking like a chip! Bless him. Can't keep my two away from the fruit bowl! Oh, is that the time? I wanted to see the head at twenty past. Got to run that thing by him, you know ...?

You: No ... what's that about?

MD: Can't say. Sorry. (*Walks away. Get me!*)

If this is what she's like when she's talking to you, you'd rather she went back to the silent treatment, at least then you won't be told that your five-year-old is a fat, thick misfit.

Back in the comfort of your bespoke kitchen/diner, you make a few calls about the design of the website you've just created, rustle up dinner for four, and pour yourself a glass of Chablis. Grown-up stuff! Your mobile bleeps twice. A text. *Hi every1 still on 4 mums nite out!!!? meeting @ worm n cabbidge 7 b their!!!! Xxxx.*

You check the clock. You can't not go. They'll all hate you. Quick. Quick. Ignore food – you'll be eating there. Time for a shower? Call cab ...? Text bleeps twice. *Not u sent that by mistake.*

How is this happening? You're 35! She's controlling you. And she can't even spell cabbage.

What she says

'My husband's bigger than yours.'
'I'll see you in the car park.'
'You smell.'

What you need to do

Get your diary and take it to the gates. Insist on liaising with her as to which days she will be blanking you. You don't want to be pencilling in blanking for Tuesday, only to find out it was scheduled for last Thursday.

Next time she deems you worthy of small talk, raise a hand and tell her: 'Do you know what, let's not bother. You don't like me. And I sure as hell don't like you.'

Spread the gossip at the school gates – she was born a hermaphrodite.

The Neigh-Boor

What he does

Fries your nerves. Everything about him from the Confederate flag on his pick-up truck to the 30ft schooner sticking out of his driveway screams crass. 'I'm here!' he announces. And within days he's cut down the cherry blossom to make way for the fleet of cars creating an oil slick on a par with the *Exxon Valdez*.

Like George Bush, he has no intention of signing up to the Kyoto Treaty. His home is lit up like a Christmas tree all year round. There are so many lasers, beams and security devices you could bring a Boeing down in his backyard.

A fairly ordinary three-bed house is not enough. He needs to erect a monument that fully glorifies his eminence. Therefore, he wastes no time in building an extension – and then an extension on that. Then a loft conversion. Then a conservatory. Then a carport, until 42 Stoat Mount is as supersized as his ego. Oh, live and let live. Well, you would, but you're at number 44. And it's semi-detached.

When he's not erecting all this nonsense, he's standing like the Colossus of Rhodes in his driveway, legs apart, arms folded, sizing up the neighbours to see if there's going to be any opposition. Don't even think about it – he's got a thick neck and loads of mates.

He thinks he's It. Ergo, you're not It. Ergo, you don't count. Ergo, he does what he likes, and 'bugger you'. At least when Tiberius flung the locals off a cliff for his own amusement, they got a dip in the Med. You'll get nothing from NB. Except contempt.

Summer twilight, the dusk chorus, church bells in the distance. You, peacefully hoeing. Abruptly, the sound of 300 car doors slamming as a horde of NB's compadres congregate in the cul-de-sac.

You: Oh God, not again.

Five minutes later. Assembled masses sweep into his backyard like bellowing wildebeest.

You: Oh God, not again.

Ten minutes later. A paraffin mushroom cloud spreads across your sycamore, forcing Midge to skitter through the catflap in alarm.

You: Oh God, not again.

Half an hour later. Shouts of 'Wahey! The rugby's on' go up as NB wheels out his nine-foot-wide high-definition plasma screen TV, complete with cinema-strength speakers.

You: Oh God, not again.

Nightfall. The thrumming of a one-million-volt generator starts up. Stoat Mount is illuminated with a light brighter than that seen at the Ascension of Christ.

You: Oh God, not again.

Midnight. You hear the cries of NB yelling, 'Stand back everyone, Big Dave's gonna blow.' The Blitz is recreated with an explosion of rockets, barrages, Roman candles, mines, fountains, Catherine wheels and sparklers.

You: Oh God, not again.

Dawn. Prising Midge off the Hessian wallpaper, while dusting your Cheerios with Diazepam.

You: Oh God, oh God, oh God.

If you do go round to make a polite petition of complaint about a) the skip that's been blocking your driveway for 16 weeks, b) the defecations on your lawn from the mini-zoo or c) his thundering tones while he conducts his business on a mobile phone millimetres from your front door, asking could he desist, perchance? you will get a) you what? b) who the hell are you? or c) where'd you spring from?

You'll point feebly at the door nary six feet from his own. He'll shake his head and walk off. At this point do not attempt to follow him to pursue the matter. You'll get a curled lip, the dismissive shoulder and the Universal Declaration of Ignorance: 'What's it got to do with you?'

What he says

'There is no such thing as society.'
'Every man for himself.'
'Like I give a ...?'

What you need to do

Keep the compadres at bay. Set up a blockade in Stoat Mount.

Spike the Earl Grey with 100-percent-proof Polish vodka at your next book club meeting until everyone's off their faces and laying into each other about the 'socio and political undercurrents in the works of Mrs Gaskell'. Make sure the bust-up spills out onto his front lawn.

Tell him you're moving out. He won't know who you are, but you can trip merrily down his block paving safe in the knowledge the next tenants will be St Jude's Charitable Institution for Deranged Strung-out Dipsos.

Conclusion

In the unlikely event you are still unsure whether your life is bedevilled with any of the aforementioned BBBs, just try this simple quiz. (NB: this has not been psychologically approved, but you know them, oh yes you do.)

1. You are standing at the office water cooler, discussing last night's episode of *The Apprentice*, when you inadvertently confuse the posh halfwit with the northern halfwit, resulting in much good-natured laughter and banter all round. Another worker approaches. Do they:
   a. assume you're talking about a real apprentice, say, 'Haven't you heard? He was found giving one of the security guards you know what in the executive loos', only to register tumbleweed silence before wheeling round to bark at you, 'In MY office, NOW';
   b. make a 'pfffft' sound, and then announce, 'I wouldn't have employed any of them. Or you lot';
   c. remain leaning on the water cooler, hours after everyone else has drifted back to their desks, until it's time for his lunch;

d. push you with one taloned finger towards a dark cupboard, hissing, 'If you ever start the post-*Apprentice* analysis before I'm ready, I will kill you';
   e. scoff, 'Sir Alan? Tough? I'd like to see him push a ten-pound baby down his birth canal. Without pethidine!'?

BBB key:

A: The PG Chimp. B: Big Rancour. C: Work to Ruler. D: Beelzeboss. E: Poacher-turned-Gamekeeper.

2 You have just delivered a best man speech to beat all others. You are Martin Luther King, Bill Clinton, Ricky Gervais. The assembled guests want an encore. Does your girlfriend:
   a. shove you hard back into your chair, warning, 'Sit! And shut it';
   b. start a subdued sobbing, which then culminates in an hysterical wail as she points accusingly at you and roars, 'Why don't YOU just marry him, then?';
   c. emerge, shrieking, from the sea of hats and Frank Ushers, brandishing the toastmaster's gavel in your direction;
   d. ignore you completely – she's too busy checking out

the port-quaffing CEO father-of-the-bride seated to her left;
e. look at you appalled, saying, 'Do you want to explain to me why you saw fit not to mention for eight years that there were six Brownie packs from the south-east of England on that scout trip'?

BBB key:

A: The Emasculator. B: The Town Crier. C: The Utter Nutter. D: The 'What's Yours is Mine' Girlfriend. E: The Interrogator.

3 You are confiding in a friend about how you don't have sex with your husband any more. Does she:
a. go and have sex with him herself at the first available opportunity (i.e., while you're going to couples therapy on your own);
b. say, 'What, ever? I can't imagine going without for that long. God, I've had the opposite problem if anything';
c. let slip a 'Yippee!';
d. sigh despondently, 'Yeah, well, they all go like that eventually. Yours just happened quicker than most';
e. shriek, 'Ohmigod! Ohmigod! OHMIGOD!'?

BBB key:

A: Commander-in-Chief. B: The Spadist. C: Miss-Fortune Teller. D: The Foul Weather Friend. E: Mag Hag.

4 You are standing at the font of St Ignatius of All the Parishes for your baby son's christening. A relative interrupts the ceremony. Do they:
   a. get struck down by a bolt of lightning emanating from the altar;
   b. say, 'I anoint this child with this chrism. In the name of the Father, and of the Son and of the Holy Ghost. Amen';
   c. mutter behind their hand, 'All those years of IVF. For that';
   d. turn on their video camera – not to record their grandson's special moment – but to show everyone footage of *them* elephant riding in Rajasthan;
   e. fall screeching from the bell tower, where they've been holed up videoing the proceedings?

BBB key:

A: The Toxin-Law. B: The Remote Controller. C: Wicked Whittler. D: Me-Me Mum. E: The Equaliser.

5 The man in your life was supposed to book you both on 'the holiday of a lifetime'. Does he:
   a. use your carefully saved cash to bid for a Darth Vader Jedi robe on eBay;
   b. tell you he will meet you at Terminal 5, Heathrow, gate 243 at 6.05 a.m. precisely on the 25th…;
   c. sign you up for Fat Camp, while he goes barracuda fishing;
   d. buy two first-class tickets for the Eros Amor Hideaway in the Maldives, complete with personal butler, private candlelit walkway to the ocean, billowing organza, tamarisk and black orchid hot pine cone massage, and frangipani sundowners. And then not speak to you for two weeks;
   e. inform you that you're both going to Cancún! Yes, you're in the Apartamente Guadalajara; he's on the other side of town in the Hotel Mayan.

BBB key:

A: The Enormous Baby Boyfriend. B: The Man from Atlantis. C: The Snake Charmer. D: The Moody Bastard. E: The 'I'm Not Your Boyfriend' Boyfriend.

6 You've just topped up your Mini Moke with unleaded at the local petrol station. Does the customer behind you at the counter:
   a. place his Tex-Mex Deluxe Ready to Go Man Meal, Ginsters pie and Tag Team Trilogy DVD directly on top of your purchases, while resting one arm on your head as he jiggles for change with the other;
   b. bawl at the cashier, 'Oi! Tiny Tim, 150 litres of your Performance Four Star. And check the tyres';
   c. announce to everyone else in the queue while you're dithering over your pin number, 'You think she'd remember an easy number like 9929, wouldn't ya?';
   d. arch an eyebrow at the scratch cards, bottle of stout and half-pound of Golden Virginia you've bought for your dad, before sending a swift text to the PTA informing them you are a feckless dipso tramp;
   e. suck his teeth as you ask the friendly cashier, 'Oh, erm, have you got any of those Poppadom crisps?' and interject over your shoulder, 'What do you think this is, the bloody Bengal Balti?'

BBB key:

A: The Neigh-Boor. B: Lord of the Manor. C: The Border Guard. D: Mummy Dearest. E: The Inconvenient Storekeeper.

Now, take a deep breath, send 'good energy' out into the universe (or look up contract killers in the Thomson local), and meditate upon these wise words:

> *'The true measure of a man is how he treats someone who can do him absolutely no good.'* (Samuel Johnson)

Here endeth the lesson …